My Land of the North

MEMORIES OF A NORTHERN CHILDHOOD

'Memories of childhood... Perhaps it's old age creeping on, but I find my mind going back to these days, to episodes in my childhood, more and more.'

CATHERINE COOKSON

My Land of the North

MEMORIES OF A NORTHERN CHILDHOOD

HEADLINE

Edited and with original colour photography by Piers Dudgeon

First published as *Catherine Cookson Country* in 1986
by William Heinemann Ltd

This revised edition first published in 1999
by HEADLINE BOOK PUBLISHING

10 9 8 7 6 5 4 3 2 1

British Library Cataloguing in Publication Data
Cookson, Catherine, 1906-1998
My Land of the North: Memories of a Northern Childhood
1. Cookson, Catherine, 1906-1998 - Childhood and youth 2. Women novelists,
English - 20th century - Biography 3. Novelists, English - 20th century - Biography
I. Title
823.9'14
ISBN 0 7472 7444 4

Printed by Tien Wah Press (PTE.) Limited, Singapore

HEADLINE BOOK PUBLISHING
A division of Hodder Headline PLC
338 Euston Road
London NW1 3BH

www.headline.co.uk
www.hodderheadline.com

CONTENTS

FOREWORD BY TOM COOKSON

Catherine at a fencing lesson in the 1930s,
around the time she first met her future husband, Tom.

'How do you do?'

'Do you fence?'

I was being introduced by my landlady to her daughter Kitty McMullen; and I can still hear those words being spoken.

The voice was strong; it was vibrant with life. I had heard nothing like it before. No, I hadn't overlooked that this girl, this woman, was beautiful; but it was the personality through the voice that was affecting me.

The next day, on a trumped-up excuse, I called her at home. Would she like to go to the pictures? Yes, she would.

From then on, the more I saw of her the more I reflected: my landlady was a working-class woman from the North East. Nothing surprising in that. Yet her daughter was living in ... no, was the owner of what had been described by the estate agent as a 'gentleman's residence'; and what is more, she spoke in a manner which, in those days, would have been said befitted such a residence. Her voice sounded cultured: she articulated correctly; there was no deliberate effort whatsoever about her pronunciation. And there was something else strange to my ear, a lilt or inflection, an inheritance from the North, that added to its charm, at least for me.

From that very first meeting we have

talked, or rather at the beginning she talked and I listened; and my admiration for her became threaded with amazement.

At University I had read Mathematics; before that, for the Higher School Certificate, I had studied not only Mathematics but also Latin and French. And perhaps from this my own reading can be gauged. But here I was, listening to a person who had left school before she was fourteen and who seemed to be consumed with a desire for learning; and (again to my surprise) to such an extent that she was wanting to discuss Voltaire's *Candide*. And yet the reason was soon apparent: she had felt herself to be alone in a fight against superstition, bigotry and intolerance. And she has never given up the fight.

It is as well to remember the period. This was the 1930's; this woman had, since she was twenty-three, been managing the laundry of Hastings Workhouse, having to supervise eleven paid staff and up to thirty inmates as well as a share of the daily casuals or tramps from the road, and at the same time she was endeavouring to run and to develop a home for epileptics.

That was the intention; but she was also willing to take a guest or two, and because, during my summer vacation, her mother had returned to the North East, I became one of those guests. To me, the work and responsibility this young woman took on was mind boggling.

And yet, somehow she found the time to write; in fact, she had been writing for some years, in any spare time she had, during her dinner break in the laundry and often, bleary-eyed, in bed at night.

One day she presented me with evidence of her efforts. I was with her on the landing of The Hurst, her 'gentleman's residence', and she opened the door of the linen cupboard and took out a number of notebooks and a stack of sheets of paper all covered with pencilled writing, and handed them to me. They were short stories and sketches of life in the workhouse; and now, looking back, I realise they were written very much in the style of her *Hamilton* series.

It should also happen that another guest was a TB patient, a man in his late thirties who, unfortunately, was soon to die, and much of his time was spent in reading and writing. Kitty had often had discussions with him, and she looked upon him as an 'intellectual', a word much used then. One day she asked him to read some of her work. It was a tentative approach she made, but behind it must have been a great longing for a few words of praise. But none was forthcoming. At that time she knew nothing about a man's egoism; her delving into Freud and Jung and the philosophies had yet to come.

Without more to do, she collected every piece of writing from that cupboard and she burned the lot. I cringe when I think of all that humour and pathos that went up in flames.

Yet this did not stop her scribbling, as she termed her writing: nothing in the world could have done that then; and certainly nothing can do that today, not even age. She carried out then, as she still does today, her own advice to would-be writers: write something every day.

In her early twenties she had read *John O'London's Weekly* and *T P & Cassell's*; she had later also read *Books & the Man* by Sidney Dark, the editor of *John O'London's*; and for her, at that time, this volume was as important as *Lord Chesterfield's Letters To His Son* had been earlier. It whetted her appetite.

We were married in June 1940, and within a month the school was evacuated to St Albans, and for the first time in her life Kitty had leisure in which to read. We had found a flat opposite the public library, and she made out a list of more than 100 titles of books she must read, over the years, of course. She would not wish me to name them: I can only say the list was a comprehensive one in that it ranged over English Literature from Chaucer to the 1920s, a list which filled me with a form of envy in that I realised just how much I had kidded myself in the past with regard to my own knowledge of literature.

As in everything else she tackles, she

persevered working through that colossal list. Even today this spirit is still exemplified in so many everyday ways: for example, she will answer all the awkward letters first. Get them out of the way, she says; maintaining that it is better to tackle obstacles straightaway, otherwise mountains invariably grow out of molehills. Most of us recite proverbs: she acts on them, and in doing so is enabled to get through an inordinate amount of work. To her, work is the essence of being; not the type of work, be it what might be termed lowly, or be it intellectual, it is work itself.

And it is this same drive probably that makes her read time and time again Plato's *Apologia* on the trial and death of Socrates, for here, she says, is someone who stuck to his principles even unto death.

And of course, the development of her character has been fully in accord with that laid out by Lord Chesterfield for his son in his celebrated *Letters*. These were grasped by her at an earlier age, and they have been her bible ever since. In bed, at night, she will still occasionally read aloud to me one of these letters; and we will discuss it, and in doing so, I, too, have come to realise the wealth of knowledge of one's fellow man, still applicable today, that can be gleaned from Chesterfield's *Letters*.

In order to press on with her reading, she kept it to a chronological order: so that after much sweating she came to the nineteenth century and the Romantic Movement poets and writers. These immediately kindled the imaginative spirit that was already present within her: she was away from the critical, reason and wit, which she hadn't fully enjoyed, and was with imagination, humour and pathos, which was to form the basis of her own writing.

Had she been born twenty or more years later than she was, she would undoubtedly have profited from the formal education that would then have been available: 'winning a scholarship' to High School, and then proceeding to

We were married in June, 1940.

University; and even being the age she is, had she been born in better circumstances in the sense that books would have been readily to hand, as well as guidance from educated people around her, she would have taken full advantage of both. In either set of circumstances, having this urge within her to write, she would, at some time, have studied the form of the novel and its development and written accordingly. But she had neither advantage, and so had perforce to be

self-educated. However, because of this her natural creativity was not channelled, as it might have been, along lines dictated by others. In consequence, she does not analyse and interpret, as the modern aspiring novelist might be guided to do, she constructs and describes through characters placed in particular environments.

In these days of advertising, she is often classified as a romantic novelist, which she certainly is not; at least in the loose way in which this word 'romantic' is today applied to novels; she is a story-teller. And one must again remember her upbringing in the years prior to and during the First World War: no wireless – this came in the 1920s – no TV; only reading, if possible; but certainly there was the listening to tales told and retold by members of the family, detailing events which had occurred much earlier, perhaps going back even to her great-grandmother's time before the 1850s. And this only child amongst adults, with her imagination and sponge of a mind, would be transposing all she was hearing into pictures.

This it was that enabled her to tell the tale, and in her own way. And she has developed this into a highly skilled talent which, today, brings pleasure, not just to thousands, but to millions of readers throughout the world, and to many of them an understanding of themselves or perhaps of their near ones. And such discerning people would deny that she is a romantic writer. Her stories do not bring in a realism in which the worst is taken for granted, but a realism in which love, caring and compassion appear, and most certainly hope. And this type of realism does exist. As well as the other. If a character struggles against the odds in order to succeed, and this is called romance, then so be it; it is but a reflection of Kitty's own life, and that has certainly been real enough.

Apart from the long years of reading, study

Left: Catherine and Tom in the garden of Bristol Lodge, Langley, where they lived in the 1980s.

Catherine receiving the Honorary degree of MA given by the University of Newcastle.

and discussion required of her in order to fit herself to write the stories that were presenting themselves to her, she still had to become conversant with the history of the nineteenth century, and to study this she was helped by those marvellous 'history story-tellers' G M Trevellyan and Arthur

'Why did I want to get away from...those grim, grimy, dock-bound river towns?'

And in the middle of the story there were these enlightening words spoken by the Duchess to her secretary: 'The first essential of a lady is to be well read and the book you must get on which to base your education is *Lord Chesterfield's Letters To His Son.'*

Oh my! What a revelation. And what an irruption those words caused in the breast of Katie McMullen, for, although she was well aware that she was bound towards a writing career, and she longed to be a writer, an amusing one, there was something she desired even more, and that was to be a lady and to speak correctly. So I flew to the South Shields library – and it was the first time I had entered a library – and I took out the tomes of *Lord Chesterfield's Letters To His Son*; and they blew me from the narrow rivulet of my existence into the broad ocean of knowledge in which I've been swimming ever since.

Yet on looking back, I seem to have been treading water all the time, for the more I read the more I learned, the wider the ocean seemed to become, and my regret now when the far bank is coming into view is I have learned so little. Yet I know that not one minute spent with Chesterfield was wasted time.

I have never wasted time, no matter how I have felt. Having now to spend a great part of my time in bed, I have to be feeling very ill indeed not to be working on a story: taping it, revising it, deleting chunks of it – a most necessary art I learnt early – or answering my mail that gets heavier every day.

Katie McMullen Country

I think this book should have been called *Katie McMullen Country*, because Katie has been writing since she was eleven years old.

Altogether, I love my husband for many reasons, one being that he made an illegitimate legitimate by giving me a name. Yet, I still wish I'd had my books published under Katie McMullen. Although that wasn't my name, not even a grandfather's name, but that of a step-grandfather, nevertheless, it is the name that holds for me all my early years. Those years that made me what I am. Catherine Cookson is merely a cloak covering the mind that developed during that raw period which harboured the inherited qualities and traits of our Kate...and of him, traits of the one at times embarrassing those of the other, but all going towards the making of Katie McMullen.

So why did I want to get away from her and my early environment? Why did I lie and deny her and it? Was it simply because of the dream that I had been fathered by a so-called gentleman? Or was it the latent artist in me striving to turn my eyes to exterior beauty and softer, wider horizons from those grim, grimy, dock-bound river towns? Or was it really to escape from Kate? ...Here, in my eighty-first year I still do not know. But what I do know is that all my hoodwinking could not cover up that girl from East Jarrow, and it took a breakdown to make me recognise her and the background that had forged her and fostered her talents.

So why didn't I give the name that portrayed my real self to this talent? Perhaps, as today, I was just so grateful to the man who gave me his name and behind whom I thought I could hide my real identity.

Perhaps a further reason why this book should have been called *Katie McMullen Country* is that, of the sixty-four books I have had published, only one is set wholly in an area outside that of the North East, that is *The Fen Tiger*, written while on a boat trip to Fenland rivers

John McMullen with Rose, me grandma, and their son, Jack. Though John was my step-grandfather, as a child in East Jarrow I was known as old John's grand-bairn.

and published under the pseudonym of Catherine Marchant.

Looked at from a distance, it seems impossible to write sixty-three stories about the same place, many set in shipyard, mining, and agricultural areas. Surely if you've read one you've read the lot? Well, there is a reason, I suppose, why I write solely about this small and esoteric part of the country, and I can best explain it by relating a true incident. I was walking along London Road in St Leonards in Sussex – I lived in Hastings for forty-six years – when I saw a lady coming towards me with a finger pointing. I didn't know her. She looked a county type: tweeds, brogues, a Henry Heath hat and a collar

'Can't you write about any other place but that North East?'

and tie. I imagined she must be looking at some-one behind me; but no, she stopped dead in front of me and, her finger still pointing, she said, 'Ah! Mrs Cookson the regional writer!' I had not before heard myself referred to as a regional writer. And then she went on in her high-falutin voice, 'I've read your books, but, you know, I've been made to wonder why you must always write about the North East. Can't you write about Hastings and St Leonards? Look at the wonderful things that have happened here, especially in

Hastings. There was the building of the castle, and the discovery of the caves; there were smugglers; and there's the fishing fleet. Not forgetting 1066, mind you! Can't you write about any other place but that North East?'

You know, it's very odd how you can come to hate somebody in two minutes flat.

I don't know what I said to that lady but I do know that when we parted I stumped away, thinking: write about any other place but the North East, I'll show her. I can write about any place I put my mind to.

So I set about proving this to the lady, who-ever she was. I got in touch with the men in the fishing fleet: I went round the boats; I learned about the wholesale buying and selling of fish; I rummaged through the ship-chandler's store. And then I set to work.

At this time I was still writing in longhand; in fact, I wrote my first sixteen books in long-hand, the writing of each one taking a year to accomplish. But one day, after having been on this story for six months, I suddenly stopped because I knew it was no good: I had to face up to the fact that the only thing in the story that had any guts was the fish. I was a regional writer; I couldn't write with any strength about any other place but that dirty backward North East, as the lady had implied.

Why?

What's bred in the bone, they say; but in my case it was what I had soaked up during those twenty-two years spent in and about East Jarrow, Jarrow and South Shields. Like a great sponge I'd taken it all in: the character of the people; the fact that work was their life's blood; their patience in the face of poverty; their perse-verance that gave them the will to hang on; their kindness; their open-handedness; their narrow-ness; their bigotry, for there were those who couldn't see beyond the confines of the county of Durham, in fact little beyond Shields and Jarrow: to many a Shields man, a Sunderland man was an enemy; and, as I brought out in *Pure as the Lily*, a North Shields man would treat a

'Like a great sponge I'd taken it all in: the character of the people.'

South Shields man as a poaching foreigner should he cross the river to look for work... And the women. Stoics would be a better name to give to the females of that time, my early time, because for most of them along those river banks it was grind in one way or another from Monday morning till Sunday night.

Of course there was the upper working class and the lower middle class. I knew them too. Did I not work for them? Only for a short period, it's true, for there was something in me that objected to servitude, that kind of servitude. And I hope my short experience with mistresses taught me how not to be one.

This, then, must be the reason why I cannot write about any other place but the North East and why this North Country idiom – I rarely use a dialect – is translated into foreign languages.

How on earth do they translate 'I'll skelp the hunger off you', or, 'He's got a slate loose', or to use stronger language, 'Bugger me eyes to hell's flames!'? But they manage to do so, and in seventeen different languages, and I'm told that every book I've written is still being published and still selling all over Western Europe. This from the child who left school when she was thirteen. At what period during that year I don't know, but after a fall in the schoolyard something happened to my hip, and there I was, free from school.

When I discovered the beauty of words
In all, I attended four schools, starting at Simonside when I was four and a half. This school was situated in what, at that time, was called the country. I was happy there; but before

North and South Shields face each other across the mouth of the Tyne, but a North Shields man would treat a South Shields man as a poaching foreigner should he cross the river to look for work.

In the novel, Pure as the Lily, *Alec Walton is deemed a foreigner by workers in Wallsend (see right) a few minutes across the Tyne from his native Jarrow: 'I almost had to swim back. When we said we'ere from Jarrow, why man, you'd have thought we'd said we'd come from Russia to start another revolution.'*

I was eight, my granda commanded that I be taken away in order 'to learn the faith'. And so for a few months I attended the Meases school at East Jarrow, before being sent to the Catholic school at High Jarrow. After a year here, I was sent to St Peter and Paul's, Tyne Dock.

What did I learn that would have gone towards making me a writer, because out of the six hours a day of education almost two were taken up with religion, and the rest, in general, with the three R's and sewing? I used to say I learnt nothing there; but I was wrong, I learnt poetry there. Miss Barrington, big Miss Barrington, kind Miss Barrington, and the younger Miss Caulfield who had taught me in High Jarrow, they both recognised that I was quick to learn poetry.

I can see myself standing on the mat on a winter's night entertaining me granda, our Kate, and likely a lodger or two, and me doing me turn:

'Had I but served my God with half the zeal I served my King, he would not in mine age have left me naked to mine enemies.'

On and on it would go. Eeh! I was clever; at least

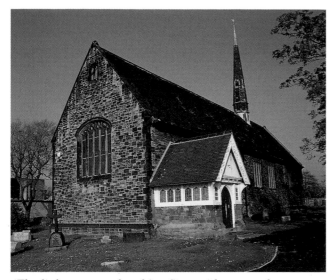

'The little country church' at Simonside, near where Catherine first went to school. In those days the country-side began at Simonside, just a short walk from where she was born.

so I had thought when Miss Barrington, pointing to the blackboard and looking at me, had said, 'Who wrote those words, Katie?'

'A fella called Shakespeare, Miss.'

Then I would follow this up on the mat with:

There was a sound of revelry by night,
And Belgium's capital had gather'd then
Her beauty and her chivalry, and bright
The lamps shone o'er fair women and brave men;
A thousand hearts beat happily; and when
Music arose with its voluptuous swell,
Soft eyes looked love to eyes which spake again,
And all went merry as a marriage bell;
But hush! hark! A deep sound strikes like a rising
*   knell!*

Yes, I did learn something at St Peter and Paul's, Tyne Dock: I learned the beauty of words, words I couldn't spell, or even understand. But there was the sound of them, the lilt of them, the pictures they conjured up in my mind. And so it was odd that, feeling for poetry as I did in those early years, my taste should waver from it, if not fall away altogether, and turn to the prose style, the story that had long lines.

Today, what I dabble in I do not call poetry but prose on short lines, because in those early years I formed an opinion of what I expect from poetry, and knew that I myself could neither aspire to produce anything acceptable to that opinion nor enjoy anything that fell below the standard instilled into me by Miss Barrington and the younger Miss Caulfield.

Making people laugh...or cry

I have been published now for thirty-seven years, and from the very beginning I have had what one would call fan mail, and it's some long

St Peter and Paul church, and school hard by (attended from 1916), are still to be found today, close to Tyne Dock Metro station. There are people in the parish who can still remember Catherine as a girl.

time now since it reached at least three thousand letters a year. But it was following the publication of my autobiography, *Our Kate*, that began the spate of so many different types of letters from so many different types of people. I imagine it was because my own life had touched on so many different aspects, including illegitimacy, drink, poverty, exploitation as a child, miscarriages, a breakdown with its myriad fears, and an inherited blood disease. This was why, I suppose, people identified with me: one or another of these things had plagued their lives too. And so, for many I became a mother confessor and, in some cases, a psychiatrist, which I must admit was heavy going...and still is, for it is difficult to answer questions when you do not know the answers.

When I read in a letter, 'I am devastated, and feel I'm going into a breakdown, because you see, I can't bear children,' I can certainly write back and say, 'My dear, I know all about that devastation,' etcetera. Yet, it's odd that I've never really brought that particular feeling into a story, because in doing so I knew I should have to show a side of me I want to forget.

I am a kind person, I wouldn't hurt a fly, in fact there was a period in my life, an intensely painful period, when even bluebottles, which I hate, would be assisted through an open window into life and liberty for their span. So how could this kind, caring, loving individual have the terrible desire to pick up a baby from a pram outside a shop and run off with it? But worse still to take hold of that baby and dash it to the ground. How often have I had to rush home to vomit and fling myself on the bed in an effort to beat this terrible urge out of me.

I lost my fourth baby in 1945 during the first year of the breakdown, and this baby syndrome kept with me for a long time afterwards, in fact, it was many years, ten, fifteen, before I could hold a child in my arms: I no longer had the desire to harm a child, but I still couldn't bear to hold one.

Oh yes, missis, I sympathise with you in being unable to bear a child.

The well-disciplined classroom of a Tyneside school of the period (1910). 'I used to say I learnt nothing at school; but I was wrong, I learnt poetry there.'

And how does one work out of a breakdown?

Yes, how does one work out of it? Those who write to me asking me for help in this way have read *Our Kate*. This account was begun in 1956, the year my mother died, but it took twelve years to complete for publication for I rewrote it eight times, deleting a little bitterness at each attempt. And so it was 1968 before it was published.

In it I describe my own breakdown, and because I had already written a number of novels, it was imagined I must have got over it.

It must therefore be depressing for them when they are told that my breakdown lasted for fully ten years and more.

During this period I read every book (dealing with nerves) that I could get my hands on, and many on philosophy because I knew that I had to try to alter my way of thinking. So I aimed, not only to write myself out of it, but to talk myself out of it. I started to give talks; I got onto

'There I was, prancing down the Queen's Road in a white linen costume... Stopping to wait for a car to pass, I looked down, and there was this full-size pink brick... I turned and looked at the Fifty Shilling Tailor's plate glass window, then at the brick again, and I had the strongest desire to pick it up and hurl it through the window.'

Woman's Hour; I was asked to 'open things'. But one thing I couldn't do, I couldn't stand up and talk, I had to sit. My excuse was I had rheumatism; you didn't own up to nerves when speaking to the WI or to Business and Professional Women in an endeavour to make them laugh...

Odd that, but my main object in life at that time was to make people happy, make people laugh...or cry. Yet for most of the time I myself was in the depths and was desperately trying to work myself out of it by physical labour: I would cut down trees, haul them to the block then saw them up – we had moved house to Loreto and started adding pieces of woodland that needed clearing – I would saw for at least two hours a day, then cart the wood into the house to keep the fires going. I also looked upon this as a form of recreation from all my other chores. In between times I cooked and I cleaned the house, did the washing...by hand – I didn't even have a dryer; I was once again saving every penny, for a certain purpose, to acquire £5,000 in order that Tom could retire early, as he was tortured with migraine. Impossible to imagine that around 1960 one could live on that amount augmented by a small pension – and, of course, I wrote.

The aim was to fill every minute so that I should not have time to think. Fourteen hours a day, seven days a week was the pattern. In between times, of course, I had to go into town to do shopping. It was then I saw the babies.

One occasion I can look back on and I can laugh about it. Being a schoolmaster's wife, I had to attend functions, such as the boys' and masters' cricket match once a year on the Central Ground. On that day, it was the aim of all wives to appear in their best bib and tucker. And I always tried to excel in this way, altering a dress or retrimming a hat. I favoured large picture hats with veils attached. I recall that I didn't want to go to the cricket match; I didn't like cricket and considered it a waste of time. But there I was, prancing down Queen's Road in a white linen costume, black shoes, black leghorn hat with veil, white gloves and a black bag. And I stopped at the Fifty Shilling Tailors. This is where I had to cross the road in order to enter the cricket field, where Tom was already playing.

Around the shop corner I noticed some men

'While talking my Northern characters down I could see them acting: I could feel through my voice their emotions, their laughter, their humour, their sorrows and their joys, *and I could catch the element of their origin, the origin that comes from far back and threads the people of this particular area.'*

attending to the brickwork and there were a number of loose bricks lying in the gutter. Stopping to wait for a car to pass, I looked down, and there was this full-size pink brick. There were bits and pieces lying around it, they didn't interest me, but that pink brick did. I turned and looked at the Fifty Shilling Tailor's plate glass window, then at the brick again, and I had the strongest desire to pick it

up and hurl it through the window.

Why? I didn't know, except that it was one of the symptoms of the breakdown: I wanted to hit out at something or someone for the life that had been dealt me up till then, especially for the fact that I'd lost God, in fact, had thrown Him out of my life, together with the Virgin: for what had they done for me and all my praying? Landed me with a breakdown. It is strange how

He also plays the part of the chauffeur, and definitely that of private secretary, for between us we see to all the fan mail and so much correspondence connected with this writing business, not forgetting the charities that take up a great deal of our time now. Our life is still made up of the seven day week and a twelve or more hour day. And besides all this, Tom can turn his hand to any household job from painting to plumbing, which is really why we have always been able to live in large houses.

If he should go first what I'll do without him God Himself alone knows, I don't. Being six years older than him I could easily will myself to join him.

In the meantime I am writing two books a year, much of it dictated on the recorder from my bed, and as I have, at the moment, nine waiting to go to the publisher, it won't matter if I never write another one.

Having reached this far, I feel I have achieved one thing at least, I have my values right.

Over the last two or three years I've received a number of honours, the latest being the OBE from Her Majesty. Previous to that in importance was the freedom of the Borough of South Shields, the Honorary degree of MA given by the University of Newcastle – I don't know who felt the more honoured, myself or Tom; he had always considered me worthy of it – then the Rotary Paul Harris Fellowship, not forgetting the Variety club of Great Britain Writer of the Year, and the Personality of The North East.

In 1968 I was awarded the Winifred Holtby Prize for the Best Regional Novel of the Year, *The Round Tower*, given by The Royal Society of Literature, and on hearing this I bawled my eyes out. And this weakness was to be my usual reaction to later recognitions.

It was in 1974 that South Shields did me the honour to make me a Freeman of the Borough. I was greatly touched by this at the time because this doesn't happen to authors. We were living in the South when this was bestowed

upon me, and I think it was from then that the urge to return crept into me. Yet I made no effort to do so; it was Tom again who thought I should come home because, as he said, if anything should happen to him I'd be among my ain folk, or, on the other hand, it would be better for me to die among my ain folk. Such an encouraging thought.

Over the years I made frequent visits back to the North East to get the feel of the setting for a new story; and so in '75 we took a house in Jesmond and, having commuted to it on five occasions within a few months, Tom, an Essex man, fell in love with Newcastle, and that clinched the matter.

There is certainly something about this area that gets people. It is fortunate in a way that we don't have it over-warm here else the two counties would be swamped.

A thing which seems to puzzle interviewers today is my having become a world famous writer – their words – without the apparent necessary university education. I should really let Tom answer this one because he waxes indignant and eloquent when he tells people that I've read more and perhaps more widely, too, than had I been to university. Of course this is biassed and an exaggerated statement, but I certainly have read a great deal; and this, as I've said so many times, stems from my reading of Chesterfield's *Letters*. What a lot I owe to that gentleman. And how amazed I was to find that everyone didn't acclaim him. Followers of Doctor Johnson, I found, openly sneered at him; so therefore I've never liked Johnson. Prejudice in its turn.

There were times during my striving to be intellectual when I would tactfully bring the conversation round to Lord Chesterfield, and some individual would counter me immediately by saying, 'Oh, Johnson said of Chesterfield that he had the manners of a dancing master and the morals of a whore.'

When this happened, and it has more than once, I have known immediately that this person

'I am still a child of the Tyne whose far horizons reached only to Palmer's Shipyard in Jarrow and the sands of South Shields.'

has never read anything of Chesterfield and, like many others, has simply picked up the quips of Doctor Johnson.

Chesterfield was a great man: first and foremost he was an educationalist; he was also a diplomat; he was a writer; he was a most eloquent speaker; he was a charmer of women. At first I accepted this trait in him because I imagined him to be a six-footer, terribly handsome, but I couldn't believe it when I first saw his picture, for he was a dwarf of a man, rather ugly, and I understood he had a high squeaky voice. Yet here was a man who could not only charm women, but also hold Parliament enthralled. And what endeared him more than anything to me was his kindness. He left evidence of this in his will. Having allotted some money to his servants he added the following words; *'These men are my*

Tyneside has changed in the last ninety years, but not as much as it did in the ninety years before that, and though there is little left today of Catherine's childhood world, what there is – be it permanence in the shape of the river Tyne itself or some building associated with her growing up or an old staithe at Jarrow Slake redolent of times past – can reward the dedicated explorer with a surprise glimpse of a spirit that was abroad in The Fifteen Streets.

equals in nature, they are only my inferiors in fortune.' Tell me of any gentleman in the eighteenth century who would voice such sentiments about his lackeys, because that's what servants were termed in those days, simply lackeys. If I loved him for nothing else I'd love him for that.

Why did he create such a fuss among the Victorians? Simply because he told his son how to deal with women, and in the nicest of terms. This, his illegitimate son, whom he sent touring the world with a tutor at seven years old, became for him a beloved pupil and he poured out his advice and his knowledge on him. And he poured it out on me too. All right, he hadn't a high opinion of women's intellect; likely, because women were clever enough to hide it in those days when men held the power, and that it was wise to know on which side you wanted your bread buttered. And he didn't like laughter. I admit that puzzled me. But then he wasn't exactly God and so was bound to have a few faults.

How delighted I am to this day when I receive a letter from a reader asking me to recommend books on Chesterfield. There have been so many written, but I think I like Willard Connely's *The True Chesterfield* best of all. Only last week a woman wrote, saying, 'Here I am seventy-six and you've opened a new world to me. Why haven't I heard of him before? And I want to answer back, 'Well, missis, you never read the romantic story by Elinor Glyn and heard the Duchess's advice to her secretary.'

Child of the Tyne

There is that word, 'romantic'. I don't like it, at least not in the sense it's tacked on to me. This didn't happen until my *Mallen* trilogy was made into a television series. Before that I was what the lady in St Leonards said I was, a regional writer. I can't imagine how anyone could tack the word 'romantic' on to *The Fifteen Streets* or *Colour Blind*, or any of the others for that matter. Of course there are the Catherine Marchant's. Yet even these, in my estimation, do not fall into the category of romantic drivel.

Why did I write under two names? people ask. Simply because in those early days *Woman's Realm* wanted me to write serials for them: they wanted romances, but with the strength of my writing and my name (because even in those early days I was, fortunately, selling well). I would write stories for them, I said, but not under the name of Catherine Cookson; and so Catherine Marchant was born. John, my agent, thought her up.

Katie Mulholland seems to be the favourite of many readers, and it isn't strange how the idea for that book was born for most of my work stems from an incident in my past.

For instance *Colour Blind*. There was a black man called Black Charlie. He used to stand on the dock bank among the men waiting to be set on the boats, and I understood he was some kind of an interpreter for the foreign sailors who came into the port. He had a family and they lived in Bede Street, somewhere up above Bob's the pawn shop, and like many another man on the bank he witnessed my shame-filled trips to Bob's as I slunk into the front shop or darted up the back lane into the cubicles. I understood he was a very nice man and was well liked. He was known as having a 'respectable family'. I recall his daughters went to St Peter and Paul's at the

same time as I did, but I cannot remember speaking to them; I can recall that in my eyes they were superior because me granda 'had a good word for Black Charlie', so he must have been all right.

I know that the family is linked, in my mind, with an incident that happened in the pawn shop. I can recall that there were two women standing in that dark well of a shop and one had put my parcel in because I wasn't of age to pawn and she had received from me a penny for her trouble. And as I was about to leave the shop she stroked my curls and said, 'Eeh! but you have bonny hair, haven't you lass.' And I, lifting my loose auburn hair aside, pointed to the dark thick rim of hair edging the bottom and back of my head, and looking up at her I said, 'That's nearly black, me Da must have been a nigger.' I

'I said, "That's nearly black, me Da must have been a nigger."'

don't know what age I was but I must have been aware that I had no Da.

Why should I say such a thing? To make them laugh like our Kate did even when she hadn't had a drink? I couldn't have been aware of the implication of my words, I only know I was pleased still to hear their laughter when I was well out of the shop.

Nevertheless, I knew at that time that there was a colour bar relating to Arabs in Corstorphine Town. A woman had just to be caught looking at an Arab and her name turned to mud. But from those days and feelings, *Colour Blind* was born.

Then *Feathers in the Fire*. Definitely this had its origin in Jackie Halliday's coal cart. Jackie Halliday sat in the middle of the cart shovelling out buckets of coal at tuppence a time. I used to think his legs were buried under the coal, and when there wasn't much coal in the cart I imagined his legs must be sticking through but that I couldn't see them. He lived in Bogey Hill, half a mile away from the New Buildings, East Jarrow. One day I was up there and, crossing a back lane, was this man, this half man moving over the cobbles on two stumps. I looked at him and he looked at me and the expression on his face was to remain with me for many years, in fact it seemed to become more vivid with time: the horror on my face must have created the anger and hurt in his. So he became the central character in *Feathers in the Fire*.

And to go back to *Katie Mulholland*. I'm never stuck for a story; before I finish one, another is forming in my mind. But I recall this day in the kitchen of Loreto in Hastings. I was talking to Tom; we were both standing in front of the Aga. We had been outside working and we had come in frozen. He had put the kettle on and we were waiting for it to boil and I said to him, 'I've got this big story in my mind but I still don't know where to place it for the best.' I had been in touch with the two Johns and they were of differing opinions about it because my original idea was to begin it in Roman times dealing with the occupation of the Wall. And I can see Tom now, lifting the kettle off the hot plate and mashing the tea as he said, 'You're always talking about Palmer's shipyard in Jarrow. Why don't you just bring the story to the last century and set it there.'

YES. YES. Of course. Palmer's shipyard, the life's blood of Jarrow for so long, and although it was now dead I could recall it vividly when it was alive. So Katie Mulholland was born.

Up till then I'd had little luck in being published in paperback. Corgi had turned me down twice – funny that, now I come to think of it, when to date they have sold well over thirty millions – and as yet I hadn't been in the American paperback market either, but a United States publisher reading this story saw how it could be adapted to paperback if, and the 'if' was big. IF it could be cut by one third.

It had been the most difficult story to write in the first place because I had done a great deal of research on Palmer's shipyard. I had been in touch with Sir Charles Mark Palmer's grandson; I had gone into Ellen Wilkinson's Politics; and in the end I felt I could speak for the working man...and also make pig iron. So the prospect of cutting it by a third daunted me. Yet everyone connected with me at this end saw the possibilities of getting into the American paperback world. And so I set about the cutting, which was much more difficult than writing the story in the first place. But it opened a new era to me: I was, so some people said, discovered.

The previous eighteen years and seventeen books I had written might never have been. And yet some of my best writing was accomplished in those years: books that I considered were the social history of the North East, readable social history interwoven into the lives of the people; and it is after all, simply the people who make history whether they are ascending to thrones or fighting wars; it is the people who create not only replicas of each other, but atmosphere, environment, and the meat for writers.

Tyne Dock from the river today.

And the people of this area have certainly provided me with the meat for my books. I may not be a Shakespeare, an Austen, a Bronte, or a Hardy, the one to whom I am often likened, but I am a product of the Tyneside and, cover me up as you may with the name of 'Cookson', gild me over with my thirty-six years in the scholastic world, OBE and MA after my name, I am still a child of the Tyne whose far horizons reached only to Palmer's Shipyard in Jarrow and the sands at South Shields. And isn't it strange that from the wider world into which I escaped I have to return, like the eel to the Sargasso Sea, to die where I began, among my ain folk.

1 MY LAND OF THE NORTH

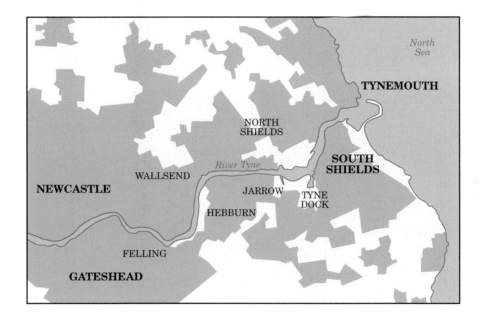

The nineteenth century saw an awesome growth in industrial activity in Tyneside, a development which attracted people to the towns from the countryside like iron filings to a magnet, the patterns of concentration roughly defining the sites of the most commercial Tyneside pits.

Among the most technologically advanced and productive coal mines in the early nineteenth century were Gateshead, Felling, Hebburn, Jarrow and South Shields, an area which forms the focal point of Catherine Cookson Country. The escalating population figures of these towns provide the scale for this incredible story of expansion and social revolution. In 1800 Jarrow's population was 1,566; in 1850, 3,835; by 1880 it had grown to 37,719. In the same years the population of South Shields grew from 11,171 to 28,292 and 55,875 respectively.

In 1841 the Royal Commission of the Employment of Children reported 'Within the last ten or twelve years an entirely new population has been produced. Where formerly there was not a single hut of a shepherd, the lofty steam chimneys of a colliery now send their columns of smoke into the sky, and in the vicinity a town is called, as if by enchantment, into immediate existence.'

The population increase due to coal mining in the early 1800s gathered pace in 1850 with the improvement of the river as an international port, the surge of activity in the chemical and glass-making industries, and the

A row of single-storey miners' cottages (each with a tiny room up in the roof), built around the middle of the nineteenth century and situated at the top of High Street, Jarrow. The idea of coal mining in Jarrow seems remote, but the visitor should not be surprised still to see sturdy ponies grazing on grass kerbs.

revolutions wrought in the ship-building and engineering industries.

South Tyneside, 1859

From a twentieth-century perspective it is almost impossible to imagine the sights, sounds and smells of this new powerhouse of activity as it was being formed.

Difficult too for Annabella Lagrange, who, being a young and impressionable member of the gentry of the nineteenth century, had been protected from the harsher realities of the industrial revolution.

Annabella had grown up in the sanctuary of Redford Hall, situated 'six miles from Newcastle and five miles from South Shields or Jarrow, depending on which path you took at the cross-roads. Its grounds extended to sixty acres, ten of which were given over to pleasure gardens, the remainder to the home farm.' There Annabella lived with her father, Edmund Lagrange, owner of a now ailing glassworks, and the woman she thought was her mother, Rosina.

In this extract from *The Glass Virgin*, Annabella is swept

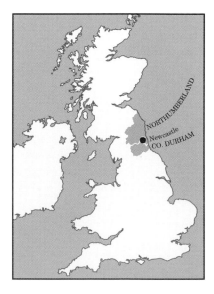

Redford Hall in the film of The Glass Virgin: *'The carriage turned out of the drive and on to the rutted road; the bumping disturbed Rosina but delighted Annabella.'*

through the south Tyneside of 1859, her experiences given a sharp edge when she is brought face-to-face with her real mother in the brothels of the Temple Town/Holborn area – that old, 'cosmopolitan' riverside stretch in which Katie Mulholland once founded a property empire and where *Colour Blind*, a novel of racial discord, is partly set. George Boston, wealthy friend of Lagrange and unwelcome suitor of Annabella, is in the carriage with them:

The carriage turned out of the drive and on to the rutted road; the bumping disturbed Rosina but delighted Annabella. She looked first to one side and then the other, and everywhere the land rolled away in open fells, showing sweeps of purple, brown and green. Then of a sudden, into her view came a huddle of make-shift shelters constructed from what looked like pieces of furniture, and scattered about them were a number of children who, on the approach of the carriage, ran towards the road.

'Oh, Mama, look! the poor children.'

'Sit back, dear,' said Rosina calmly.

Annabella sat back but she could still see the children running along the high bank keeping apace of the carriage. They were all bare-foot, and like the three distant children in her memory they were dirty and gaunt and none of them were laughing.

'Then of a sudden, into her view came a huddle of make-shift shelters...and scattered about them were a number of children who, on the approach of the carriage, ran towards the road.'

Edmund Lagrange now shouted to his coachman, 'Speed her up there!' Then in an undertone to Boston he said, 'Rosier's rabble; another strike. It took the militia to get that lot out; he's filled the village with Irish. There'll be serious trouble one day, mark my words. He can't handle the men, never could, neither he nor his father.' He spoke as one who could handle men.

Two miles further on they passed through Rosier's village. The dust flew up from the horses' hooves and smothered the women standing at the doors of the row of cottages.

There were children here, too, standing at the side of the road and some of them waved and shouted, and Annabella had the desire to wave back, but knew she mustn't.

Another two miles further on and they entered Jarrow, and Annabella was again sitting on the edge of the seat.

In the past ten years Jarrow had emerged from a pit village and a small boat building community into a bustling, overcrowded town in the making. Two men out of every three had an Irish brogue; fighting and drinking were the order of the day; and the reason for the prosperity that enabled working men to drink frequently was the birth of Palmer's shipyard.

In 1850 there had been between two hundred and fifty and three hundred houses in Jarrow; now in 1859 there were three thousand and builders were working like mad grabbing at the green fields to erect row on top of row of flat-faced single bricked dwellings.

The carriage tour was to take in Palmer's shipyard, so they emerged into Ellison Street, so named after a man who owned a great deal of the land there-abouts. And the horses going at a spanking pace along the street brought women from the communal taps at the corner ends, customers out of shops, and even turned men's heads from their beer drinking to crowd at the public

'The carriage tour was to take in Palmer's Shipyard.' Palmer's was the magnet of change on Tyneside in the 1850s.

house windows and ask, 'Is it Palmer?' and hear the reply, 'No. Bloody gentry; bloody blood-suckers.'

When they reached the gate of the steelworks, Edmund Lagrange called a halt to the coachman; then standing by the side of the carriage door, he pointed out the great smoking chimneys, the mass of towering iron that was the gantries and cranes, the ships in the river hugging the staithes, and, of all things, a big, black looking boat sailing down the river with the smoke pouring out of a funnel in the middle of her as if the whole erection was on fire.

The wonder of it all struck Annabella dumb, but not pleasingly so. In her ten years the only place she had visited outside the perimeter of the grounds was Durham, and Durham was different from Jarrow; it had a wonderful cathedral standing on a rock towering over the river and it was very imposing and everything looked clean, except some of the men who were usually covered in coal dust and who, she understood, were miners. But this Jarrow, this was a different world; the great ships, the noise, the men scurrying about like ants, and the crowds in the streets all dressed in dark, drab clothes. She had noticed a dreadful thing outside one of the inns; she had actually seen a woman lying in

South Shields, 1890. 'The town seemed full of poor children, the whole world seemed full of barefoot children. Of course, the weather was warm; perhaps that was why they were without shoes or stockings.'

the gutter...

The carriage turned round and once more the horses were galloping down Ellison Street with children running on each side of the carriage now, shouting in what sounded like a foreign language.

'Hoy a ha'penny oot!'

When no money was forthcoming the words, still unintelligible, took on a derisive tone.

'Gan on, ya big gob skites!

'Aal dressed up like farthin' dolls.

'Sittin' up a height like bloody stuffed dummies.'

When Armorer's whip licked along one side of the carriage the children shied away, except one who yelled up at him, 'Go on you fat-arsed lackey. come doon offa that an' Aa'll rattle your cannister for you. Go on, ya stink.' The boy hung on to the door of the carriage now and yelled at the company. 'Ya all stink; ya rift up me belly like a bad dinner.'

All this while Edmund Lagrange had been talking to George Boston as if the carriage was running through open deserted country and Rosina sat straight-backed, her eyes directed towards the coachman; but Annabella and Stephen stared at the children, Stephen with an amused smile on his lips, and Annabella straight-faced and troubled, especially when Armorer kept using his

Looking from the ruins of Bede's monastery towards the River Don.

Tyne Dock, 1890, past which Edmund steered Annabella towards Temple Town on the pretext of showing her the ships; the girl unaware that she was about to set eyes on her true mother.

whip.

The carriage now passed the expanse of land where disused salt pans lined the banks of the River Don; it passed the church where St Bede had preached and taught; it crossed the river by a stone bridge, then on past the Jarrow Slacks, and down the long country road with farms and fields on one side and the River Tyne on the other, and so into Tyne Dock, where on the third of March in that very year the new docks had been opened.

Edmund Lagrange pointed derisively at the huge gates as they passed and remarked to George Boston, 'A white elephant if ever there was one; a new dock and the river so silted up you can walk across to North Shields at low tide! It's ludicrous, don't you think? Then they grumble about Newcastle getting all the shipping. Ten years they've been making that dock; you would have thought the '54 business would have deterred them, but no, somebody got an idea and they must carry it through.'

Rosina looked at her husband as he talked. Anyone who didn't know him would think that he had the town and its affairs at heart. His reference to '54, which Mr Boston likely knew nothing about, was the terrible day when sixty-three ships which were seeking refuge in the river were wrecked and many, many lives lost, and all in sight of people standing on the shore. But Edmund didn't really care if the town sank or swam; he talked to impress Mr Boston,

and there could be only one reason why he wanted to impress this young man, for Mr Boston was a common man and ungainly in both manner and speech. She wondered to what extent her husband was in this young man's debt and what hope Mr Boston held out of being repaid.

Her eyes widened a little when her husband now directed the coachman away from the main road which led into South Shields and along by the river through what she knew to be a most disreputable area which led to The Gut and finally to the Market Place. When he gave further instructions that Armorer should walk the horses she felt a protest rising in her but checked it before it escaped her lips. Annabella, she felt, had seen enough of sordid living for one day, but what she had witnessed in Jarrow would be nothing to what she would see if they went through Temple Town, which was obviously where Edmund was directing the carriage.

Armorer, too, was obviously surprised at his master's orders for he repeated, 'Through Temple Town, Sir?'

'Yes, yes; we'll see more of the river that way, and the ships.' He turned to Annabella. 'You'd like to see the ships, wouldn't you?'

'Yes, Papa.'

But she didn't see the ships for some time. What she saw were rough

The ruins of the monastery 'where Bede had preached and taught'. The Venerable Bede lived and worked here between 682 and 735 AD, making the monastery a spiritual focus for Christians in Western Europe. The ruins may still be seen. Behind – see the tower – lies the church of St Paul's Jarrow; its chancel (founded in April 685) is the same one in which Bede worshipped. Here, too, Catherine received her first Communion.

'Annabella, she felt, had seen enough of sordid living for one day, but what she had witnessed in Jarrow would be nothing to what she would see if they went through Temple Town.'

looking people, poor people, and lots of children, and mostly bare-footed. The towns seemed full of poor children, the whole world seemed full of bare-foot children. Of course, the weather was warm; perhaps that was why they were without shoes or stockings.

Sometimes she herself longed to take off her shoes and stockings and run in the grass with her feet bare, that is, when it was warm; but perhaps these children had no shoes and stockings on when it was cold, wet, snowing. She said to no one in particular, 'They have no shoes or stockings on,' and her papa answered, 'They don't need them, my dear; the soles of their feet are like leather.'

'Really!' She moved her head from side to side and smiled slightly at her father. His answer was very reassuring.

But the further the carriage went into the old town the more she became aware of the drabness, the dirt, the stench. All the people were odd looking. Perhaps, she surmised, they were from foreign lands. Then an awful thing happened; she saw a lady empty a chamber pot from an upstairs window and Armorer had to jerk the horses into a gallop to avoid the contents. She was amazed that the lady had aimed the filth at them and that she continued to

Tyne Dock and East Jarrow, 1906

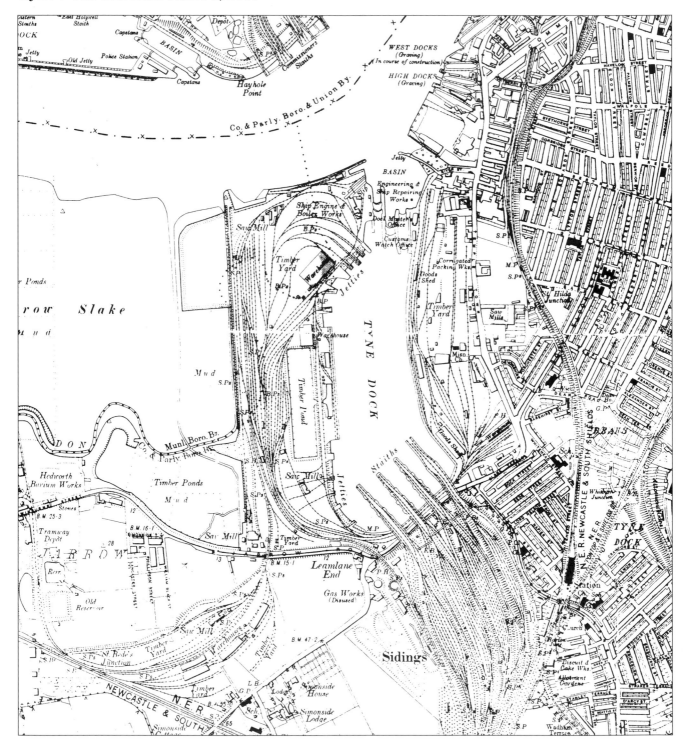

Below right: The little girl is standing across the road from 5 Leam Lane where Catherine was born in 1906, at the point where Leam Lane funnelled out on to the Jarrow Road.

Today (see below), Leam Lane is the A194 dual carriageway and Catherine's birthplace a petrol station. There is a plaque nearby.

Left: The map shows Leam Lane and Tyne Dock, with its great staithes over four of the five slime-dripping arches, and the Jarrow Slake, where Christine and Katie met their end in The Fifteen Streets.

Off the map are Palmers, further west along the Jarrow Road, and St Bede's monastery, in the south western corner of the Slake. The New Buildings, where Catherine moved in 1912, is the island community just south of the Jarrow Road. Temple Town, where Annabella met her mother, can be seen on the east side of Tyne Dock.

laugh aloud. Looking at her mama after this incident she saw that her face was very white and her mouth tight, as when she was angry. Her father swore, but Mr Boston laughed and when she looked at Stephen she was surprised that he, too, was almost laughing.

They now entered a street named Crane Street. It was facing the river and she didn't know whether to look at the ships or towards the pavement for a lady was walking in step with the carriage. She was different from all the other ladies she had seen because she was wearing gay coloured clothes. The lady was looking at her, staring at her, and when they were some way down the street the lady smiled, and she smiled back at her, then her gaze was diverted

from the lady to a high window where there were a lot of ladies, and they were hanging over the sill and shouting. All their faces looked merry and happy and she saw her papa look up at them and smile slightly, and so did Mr Boston. But her mama was looking at the lady who was walking by the carriage; but the lady wasn't looking at her mama, she was looking at her. She had never seen a lady before with such a colourful face, her eyes were very dark and her lips and cheeks were very red...

The Glass Virgin

Between the era described above in *The Glass Virgin* and 1906 the population in Northumberland grew from 300,000 to 600,000; in County Durham it increased from 390,000 to 1,190,000 in the same period of fifty years.

I was born on June 10th, 1906, in Number 5 Leam Lane, at the bottom of Simonside Bank, Tyne Dock. Tyne Dock is, or was at the time, just what it says, a dock on the river Tyne. Where the river flows into the North Sea the towns of North and South Shields

Since the coming of the railway and the dredging of the Tyne in the 1850s, both banks of the river had changed beyond recognition. A multiplicity of railway lines now snaked their way over four of the five slime-dripping arches at Leam Lane end on to the great dock staithes, and as Catherine lay in bed at night she could hear the horns of ships and the creaking and groaning of shunting trains. She was indeed a child of the Tyne.

Right: The great Tyne Dock arches are no more, though the vicinity is known as The Arches.

stand, one on each bank. South Shields is connected with Tyne Dock; up river Jarrow, Hebburn, Pelaw, Felling and Gateshead all follow; on the other side of the river is North Shields, then follows Howdon, Wallsend, Willington Quay and Newcastle. Both banks were lined

'One day when I was five, and walking through the arches from the Docks I saw someone coming towards me who apparently I didn't want to meet for I crossed over the road and, turning my face to the blank, black wall, walked sideways until I had passed them, for I knew that if I couldn't see them they couldn't see me. I was to follow this pattern for many years. I would turn my face to a wall; and always I would see a picture, which became the focal point of my striving. It showed me a big house peopled by ladies and gentlemen... Of course, I was in the picture, dead centre.'

with shipyards, chemical works and factories.

Simonside Bank was just a cluster of houses within three minutes walk, under five great slime-dripping arches, of the actual dock gates; and yet we were on the verge of what was known as the country. A few minutes walk up the hill from our house were the big houses. There were about half-a-dozen of them, and above them a farm and a little country school and church.

The first group of houses on the left going up the bank, was confined between two house-shops, one at each end. One was kept by the Lodges, the other by the Lawsons. In the middle was a public house. I never knew it called anything but 'Twenty-seven', because I understand there were only twenty-six staithes in the docks and the bar being a place where the men eventually docked became twenty-seven. Our house was next to the bar. On the opposite side were two houses and a blacksmith's shop.

I must have been between five and six when we moved from Leam Lane to East Jarrow. We made the move on a flat cart. It would likely be Jackie Halliday's, for he was the coalman and the only one we knew who had a cart. And I remember I sat on the back, under

'What's yours?'

'That sleeper.'

'The whole slack's yours!' She looked down on me with her round piercing eyes.

I didn't dispute this but said, 'It is mine. I pulled it out an' just left it, I was comin' back for it.'

There followed a verbal battle which I must have won, for with the sack over my shoulder and pulling the sleeper by the piece of rope I went home, and me granda, seeing it was a nice piece of wood,

Left, above and right: Tyne Dock today, nearly half a century after Catherine's stories began to pass into the folklore of the place. It may not be as busy as it once was, but if the novels tell us anything it is not to idealise its heyday. After two centuries of industrialisation, there is, as ever, change afoot.

used it to renew a post of the hen cree, without bothering to take the staple out.

Morgan, the policeman who lived in the Hall, wasn't exactly loved by the people in the New Buildings and he was hated by me granda. One day we had a visit from him. He was looking for sleepers; a number of them had been cut away from the timbers, and this was serious as the timbers drifted apart and took some getting together again. And there facing him, with the staple for proof, was a sleeper.

Eventually there was a summons and me granda had to appear in Court. It was a dreadful state of affairs. It was the first time me granda had been in Court in his life, which was surely a miscarriage of justice, and this occasion, being innocent and indignant, he absolutely refused to plead guilty and they were for sending the case to the Assizes, for as the Magistrate said, 'How could a child of eight years carry such a piece of wood as this?' – the sleeper was no longer in the hen cree but now reposed on the bench before him. To this me granda replied, 'You don't know me granddaughter, sir.'

The South Shields ferry today, docking at Ferry Street, just west of the Market Place.

Jarrow, 1900. 'The greatest excitement that I had in coming back to the North was crossing on the ferry from Shields to North Shields. I looked up the river and there were the cranes and all the ships; it was busy then.'

Catherine Cookson Countryside

ANOTHER FACE OF MY LAND

My land of deep lakes
With mountain shadows
Like ancient cities
Buried and at rest in their depths.
My land of hidden valleys
Dotted with homesteads,
Solitary, aloof.
My land of barren fells,
Scree slopes gripped by hooves of sheep
And rams, protective of their own.
My land of skies stretching to infinity,
Blue high sheets of sheer clear light.
My land of mists,
Grey, wet, body-soaking mists
That shroud you to a trembling halt.
My land of tones
Fan-lit and sombre,
Heather purples and autumn golds.
Winter white,
Black frost laden nights
Driving hard to spring
And new born grass
And released water
Rushing from its prison of ice.
Oh, my land of sturdy men,
Short, stumpy men in part,
And women, warm of heart
And worth
And laughing lips,
My land of the North.

'A brake trip was often the only holiday that two-thirds of the population of the New Buildings ever had... they would be right into the country to some place where there was woodland and a stream.'

The rich variety of scene provided by the countryside of both County Durham and Northumberland Catherine, as a child, knew little of, even though it had begun just a walk away from East Jarrow. Later, however, it became a significant element in the inspiration of her fictional characters.

She looked at me impatiently. 'Oh, come on,' she said, straightening her apron and clicking her tongue.

Her attitude didn't dampen my spirits and I danced before her up the street into the wood. Then from my vantage point I stopped, and when she came and stood by my side I pointed and she looked. Then her hand came slowly round my shoulder and she pressed me to her.

And as we stood like this, gazing spellbound at the first sprinkling of anemones, I said, 'They seem glad to be out, Mam, don't they?' Her hand drew me closer and she said, 'Yes, hinny, they're glad the winter's over.' Then much to my surprise she didn't turn homeward but walked quietly on into the wood, her arm still around me.

At one point she turned and looked back, and I did, too, wondering what she was looking for. Then she did a strange thing. She went down on her hunkers like my dad did and, taking me by the shoulders, she gazed into my face, her eyes moving around it as if looking for something, like when I've had a flea on me, and pressing my face between her large, rough hands she exclaimed softly, 'Oh, me bairn.' Then she said a thing that was stranger than her kneeling, yet not so strange, for I understood it in part. 'Keep this all your life, hinny,' she said. And she ended with something which contradicted a daily statement of hers, for she said, 'Never change. Try to remain as you are, always.'

Fenwick Houses

Right: Families ready for an outing to Shotley Bridge. 'Hoy a ha'penny oot!' the children would be screaming and yelling as they ran after the brake, and there were ha'pennies and pennies thrown at them.

I was ten years old when I first accompanied my mother, Kate, on a brake trip. There would be brake trips every year, and these trips wouldn't be to the seaside, they would be right into the country to some place where there was woodland and a stream.

A brake trip was often the only holiday that two-thirds of the population of the New Buildings ever had. Somebody would get up

'Even in winter Davie always paused at this spot to breathe in the air; it seemed purer from up here... It was almost as good, he considered, as the air you breathed from the top of Shale Tor.'   *Feathers in the Fire*

Feathers in the Fire was one of the first of Catherine's novels to be set away from Tyneside and there is a marked imaginative gain from the harsh countryside in which it is set. The novel's evocation of chill, wild, high up, wide open spaces calls to mind a day in Catherine's childhood when her mother, Kate, conjured up a similar image in song. Mother and daughter were working silently at a weaving frame in the kitchen of William Black Street when Kate began, in a very soft, quiet voice, to sing her favourite song, Thora, a traditional song of the North. She sang it with such feeling that Catherine remembered the occasion to the end of her life, even recording the song in 1996. Catherine's relationship with Kate was always fraught, but it was the Kate in her that found expression in her work, and Kate's mythic, snow-covered Land of the North, with its stars and magic skies, is a haunting echo of the heroic yet tragic image of Northernness evoked by so many of Catherine's novels:

I stand in a land of roses,
But I dream of a land of snow,
Where you and I were happy
In years of long ago.
Nightingales in the branches,
Stars in the magic skies,
But I only hear you singing,
I only see your eyes..

I stand again in the Northland
But in silence and in shame.
Your grave is my only landmark
And men have forgotten my name.
'Tis a tale that is pure and older
Than any sages tell.
I loved you in life too little,
I love you in death too well.
Speak, speak, speak to me Thora,
Speak from your heaven to me,
Child of my dreams,
Love of my life,
Hope of the world to be!

The McBain farm in Feathers in the Fire *lies west of Whitfield and south of Plenmeller Common. See the map, page 60.*

From where he, Davie, stood he could see a great expanse of land beyond the boundary of the farm. To the right of him were hills, young mountains some of them; showing green and brown, with here and there great black patches, telling scars of dead lead mines. To the left the land rolled into moorland flatness on its way to Haltwhistle and the South Tyne. In front of him, eight miles as the crow flew, twelve miles by the twisting road, lay Allendale in its nest of moors.

Feathers in the Fire

Looking south from Plenmeller Common towards Whitfield Moor. 'From where he, Davie, stood he could see a great expanse of land beyond the boundary of the farm. To the right of him were hills, young mountains some of them...'

*Looking north towards Plenmeller.
'To the left the land rolled into
moorland flatness on its way to
Haltwhistle and the South Tyne. In
front of him, eight miles as the
crow flew, twelve miles by the
twisting road, lay Allendale in its
nest of moors.'*

*Looking up to the top of the Tor,
where the cripple, Amos, appears
with his half-sister, Jane.*

In 1981 Catherine and Tom bought Bristol Lodge in Langley village (left), a move that intensified the influence of the spirit of rural Northumberland on her work. Langley village emerged in the 18th century around a mill used for smelting lead ore mined over Alston Moor. The lake (see right), which met their garden on the far bank and inspired the magical lakeside scenes in The Moth, *together with the disused railway and smelting works in nearby woodland (see below right) and a 30m-high chimney connected to the old mill by means of a mile-long flue (see below), all attest to the industry on which the village once subsisted. In* A Dinner of Herbs *the strange, witch-like herbalist, Kate Makepeace, is a personification of the hard, unyielding lead-mining country in which she and of course Catherine dwelt. The film of* The Dwelling Place *was also located up here.*

The Tor in *Feathers in the Fire* was set just at the back here, but Jackie Halliday was the real reason I wrote that story.

Jackie Halliday used to sell coal, tuppence a bucket, off a flat cart and I thought his legs were buried in the coal. As a child, I didn't work it out that I should have seen them sticking through the cart.

Then one day I went up Bogey Hill – I very rarely went up Bogey Hill – and I saw this 'thing' going across the back lane and I recognised his face and it was Jackie Halliday and for the first time I realised that the man had no legs, and I stopped and stared at him.

Well, a child's horror can affect someone, and I saw it in that man's face. And for years when a tragedy came up or someone was hurt very badly by someone else – not necessarily physically – I recalled the look on that man's face. It was misty: the face had gone but the feeling remained. And I felt that I had to portray that in some way, I felt that I was really experiencing what Jackie Halliday must have felt when as a young man he found that he had no legs. Just imagine...in a tough area like the Tyne, where they are all he-

men. It seemed so unfair, but then ask yourself, is there anything fair in Nature? Ask yourself, when a mountain can come down and bury people in its mud. Is there anything fair in Nature, when a volcano can burst and burn people to death? Is there anything fair?

Here Amos appears on the Tor with his half-sister, Jane.

The sky was endless, seemingly without horizons. The bracken on the right of the Tor was shoulder high, some already tinged yellow, forerunner of the reds and purple that would turn the fells and hills into a warm flame. At the foot of the Tor were clusters of bilberry bushes, their fruit standing out like black and purple stains, and she pointed this out to the boy. But he didn't seem interested, for his gaze was directed to the top of the Tor.

The easiest way up was through the bracken, but the child would be enveloped in it, the fronds would impede him, and they could easily cut, so she led the way along the narrow road that skirted the foot of the Tor on the north side, where it was mostly shale, giving place to rough rock. Starting from the road was a path, cut diagonally, and slowly mounting its way to the summit, and she took this. Picking Amos up in her arms with the order for him to hang onto his crutches and not get excited for fear he overbalanced them both, she began to

ascend. The end of the path was out of sight on the east side of the Tor and away from the road, and when she finally reached it, she dropped the boy to the ground, then sat down on a rock and, panting and laughing, said, 'Well, here we are.'

The child was standing supporting himself on his crutches. She stared at his face; it was wearing the strangest expression. He was looking towards Whitfield Moor and the hills beyond. She watched him look from one side to the other, taking in the great range of space; then his head went slowly back on his shoulders and he gazed up into the sky.

'Isn't it beautiful?' She put out her arm and encircled his waist, and he turned and looked at her and smiled. And he was beautiful too. This face often made her sad, but not today; it was as if she also, like him, were seeing the world outside the farm for the first time. She gripped him to her and he dropped his crutches, and as she had been wont to do since she was a small child, until she was twelve years old, she rolled on the grass, but now with him pressed tightly to her. When she stopped they lay, their faces close together, laughing; then like an eel he was away from her, scrambling over the grass on all fours, his body, from waist to hips, wobbling from side to side. When he reached his crutches he began to run wildly here and there like someone demented, and she

The village of Elmholm in The Girl *also has strong links with the Allendale lead-mining industry. Below, the nearby Killhope mine.*

Scars left when the industry died in the 19th century still abound. Below, Langley Castle inspired the Peel House in The Girl.

chased him, laughing as she called, 'Amos! Amos! Stop! Keep away from the edge! Be careful. Be careful.' Every time her hands went to grasp him, he ducked or slithered from her hold.

The agility on his new-found legs amazed her; it was as if he had used the crutches from birth. It seemed that Parson Hedley was right, he was going to be very adaptable. Parson Hedley said he was the brightest child he had ever come across. For a moment a cloud passed over the bright day as she thought, if only her father could see him as Parson Hedley saw him; or for the matter, if her mother had viewed him as a human being; if only one of them had taken him to their hearts. Anyway, he had her, he would always have her.

She lifted up her skirts and raced towards him, for now he was some distance away and nearing the edge of the Tor where it dropped almost sheer to the road below. This part was strewn with loose rocks and boulders and, as he went twisting in and out of them, she had a job to outmanoeuvre him. When at last she caught him, she sat down with her back to a boulder and laughed as she rocked him. Then quite suddenly, as he was apt to do, he asked a most disconcerting question, 'Why haven't I got legs like you, Jan?' He sat back from her straight up on his buttocks, then with a swift movement he lifted her skirt and petticoats back to her knees.

'Amos!' Her voice held a sharp note. 'You mustn't do that.'

'Why?'

'Well, just because.'

'But why have you got legs and I haven't?'

'You...you had an accident.'

'When?'

'Oh.' She closed her eyes and swallowed. 'It was before you were born.'

'What...what kind? Did I fall?'

'No.'

'Well, what kind of accident?'

'You...you mustn't ask such questions.'

'Why?'

She couldn't say to him 'because she didn't know the answers', for he expected her to know all the answers. She was saved from further embarrassment by the sound of a pony trap below them. It was coming around the bend of the road. Jumping to her feet and pulling the boy with her, she raised her hand and shouted, 'Parson Hedley! Parson Hedley!'

The man in the trap stopped and looked about him, then lifted his head. She waved down to him again, and at this he waved back, then he lowered his

Catherine envisaged Elmholm – the village in The Girl *– as being between Allendale Town and Sinderhope, although Simonburn on the North Tyne (above and right) was chosen as film location. Below right: the church where Hannah Boyle married Fred Loam and the vicar handed her the sealed envelope, revealing that Hannah was not, after all, Matthew Thornton's daughter.*

hand and stared at the small figure by her side, and she knew that he was very surprised at what he was seeing. She put her hand to her mouth and shouted, 'We'll come down.' And at this he called back, 'No, stay there, I'll come up; just let me fasten Toby.'

She watched him drive the trap to where the ground levelled off sufficiently for him to take it off the road and where there was grass for the pony to nibble; then she followed his movements as he made his way up the winding path, and when he was below them, she laughed down at him. Then with Amos stumping by her side, she ran back towards where the path came out on the summit. They reached the spot simultaneously and their greetings were high and pleasurable as if they hadn't met for some long time, instead of twenty-four hours previously.

The parson was a man of medium build. He had flat rather blunt features, none of which had any claim to good looks, except perhaps his eyes; even these were nondescript in colour, being of a flecked grey. But it was the eyes that gave the interest to the face; perhaps it was kindliness and understanding in their depths, and a certain sharp keenness in their glance, which rarely held censure, that made them attractive.

He gazed down at the boy who had become a deep interest in his life, as also had his sister, but whereas he could express his feelings on the former, he had to hide them on the latter. For all her capabilities, he still considered Jane a child, and even if she hadn't been, there remained circumstances which prevented him from presenting himself as anything but a friend, pastor, and tutor. But with the child it was different, and now he exclaimed loudly, 'Well! Well! A day of miracles. What is this?' He stood back and surveyed the boy standing erect, shoulders hunched, on the small crutches; and when Amos, in his forthright manner, stated, 'I've got legs,' he had to pause before answering, 'Indeed, indeed you have, Amos. Now why didn't we think of this before, eh Jane?'

Jane smiled widely at him. 'That's the very thought that came to me a short while ago, Parson. Perhaps it's because I thought he couldn't manage them...'

'I can manage them, look, look,' Amos interrupted while he demonstrated, going round in small circles, and she laughed as she caught him, crying, 'We can see. Yes, darling, we can see. But you'll make yourself dizzy. Come along, sit down.'

When they were seated on the grass, Arnold Hedley gazed before him for a moment in silence, and then said, 'It's years since I was up here; I'd forgotten how magnificent was the view.' Then glancing at the boy who was sitting to the side of Jane, he said low, under his breath, 'It was good for him to see the world for the first time from this spot. It was like you to think of bringing him up.'

'It wasn't my idea, Parson, it was Molly who suggested it.'

He looked into her face. She was so honest, she would not even take a little credit herself when it rightly belonged to someone else. Her face to him was beautiful, for it held the beauty of honesty, the beauty of an unselfish nature and a kindly heart. True, she was given to bouts of temper, but then she was but human. And she was young, so young, too young to have the responsibility of mothering this boy and running that disembowelled tortured household. He was often amazed at the gaiety she managed to maintain. But then her charge, although terribly handicapped, was a lively, intelligent little fellow, too intelligent, he considered at times, for his age. But he supposed God in His wisdom had given

him the gift of memory and keen perception to make up for his lack.

He was bending forward towards Jane to make a further comment when he was pushed aside by Amos's roughly forcing himself between them from behind. The force levelled by the child's arm in his ribs was of a strength one would associate with a boy of ten or twelve. He held back his head and surveyed the child as Jane admonished him, saying, 'That's naughty, Amos. You mustn't push like that. That's very naughty.'

Amos was now sitting upright between them. There was a slight smile on his face, and with a lightning movement he turned to the parson, raised his hand, and viciously nipped the lobe of his ear.

When Arnold Hedley actually cried out with equal amounts of surprise and pain, Jane, snatching the boy's hands, slapped them hard as she cried, 'That's very wicked, Amos, very wicked. How dare you!'

Amos stared wide-eyed up at her, and, his smile sliding into a grin now, he said, 'He pulls my ear.'

She exchanged a glance over his head with Arnold; then she swallowed and said, 'Parson does it playfully, he never hurts you. There is a difference between pulling and nipping. If you ever do that again, you'll get a sound smacking, a real smacking.'

Each season strikes a different character up on the fells.

The smile slid from the boy's face, his eyes clouded, and his lips fell firmly one on the other. In another child of similar years this might have been a prelude to tears, but he showed no signs of crying; instead he threw himself forward onto his hands and knees, crawled swiftly to where his crutches were, stood up on them and, looking from one to the other, said firmly, 'I'm going down to the farmyard.'
Feathers in the Fire

When I left the North in 1929 I knew nothing of this particular part of my land. I had been half a dozen times to Newcastle, once to Durham, once to Gilsand, a few times to Birtley. My horizon encompassed Jarrow and Shields, and even in these places I knew only main streets. I existed mostly in the circle of Tyne Dock and East Jarrow.

My first job was in a workhouse in Tendring, Essex, and what I saw of the countryside there left me cold. Suddenly this girl, who had come from this industrial area where even at night-time you heard the horns of the ships and the background noises of the shunting trains, found herself in the midst of this desolate countryside. In fact it wasn't desolate, it was all farmland: a vast expanse of flat farmland; it was like a different country and I was so lonely. I was stuck there for nine months and I hated it.

And I think that feeling has stayed with me. There's nothing pleases Tom more than to walk through a field; Tom loves flat Essex and also the fenland. We had a boat on the fens and those flat expanses nearly drove me mad.

But up here in the hills I know that I am in my own country, not soft like the downs nor flat like the fens. This countryside is raw, and it is with me and I feel it. Tom must be tired of the times we have brought the car from Hexham to Langley and I have said that it is the most beautiful sight that I have ever seen. As you approach the 'top', as we call it, you can look across and see that you're surrounded by hills, and Langley seems to be in a great valley, and all the way, everywhere you look, there are hills coming down, all the way round, coming down to this valley.

I first became afraid of hills up here when Tom took me up Shap Fell and over Alston. We were travelling by car from Loreto, the house where we then lived in Hastings, to my cousins in Birtley, in Durham, because I had been asked again and again to give a talk to a group of Women's Institutes.

Before, when visiting the North to seek out localities for my stories, and also to give talks, I had travelled by train, but this time there we were in the car and Tom, as always, took the longest way round in order that we could see the beautiful scenery of Northumberland. I found myself heading for what I didn't know then was the great, great expanse of Alston moors.

Tom took Catherine over Hartside Top, almost 2,000 feet above sea level, an exhilarating ride in good conditions. Readers of The Mallen Streak *will recognise the 'great fall' from the edge of the car as the cliff where Thomas Mallen's illegitimate son, Donald, a dark, brooding character given to long silences and bursts of temper, is killed by his consumptive half-brother, Matthew. There are many such places on this road from Penrith.*

'At different times in my life I knew when I had been any place that had a deep fall to the side I had the most strange feeling, sometimes touching on terror.'

The 'wreck of an old house', which Catherine describes finding during her 'day of terror', became a place of refuge for Matthew and Constance Mallen, a significant moment in The Mallen Streak.

At different times in my life I knew when I had been any place that had a deep fall to the side I had the most strange feeling, sometimes touching on terror. But what I experienced that day went past terror. Tom drove over the hills, up, up, into this space that went on for eternity, the heights and everything about it found me crouched on the floor of the car beside the seat. I was shaking with terror from head to foot. All I could gasp was, 'Get out of this!' On and on he went, aiming to get out of it of course, by reaching the end of it. At one time he stopped the car and said, 'Look, try, try to sit up and look about you. It's the most magnificent sight.'

I couldn't answer, my heart was racing so fast. My pulse was racing so fast that it is a great wonder to me now that I didn't have a heart attack.

'Just lift your head,' he begged, 'or look through the windscreen. Just lift your head.'

I managed to raise my head from my huddled, crouch position and look through the windscreen, and there I was confronted by a fly moving slowly, slowly upwards. I followed it. I followed its progress until I realised it wasn't a fly, it was a car in the far, far distance, mounting the rise, and I let out a scream and once more my head was buried.

So on and on he drove until we ran down into some sort of a village, and he dragged me out of my cramped position and I sat on the footboard and I was sick. 'I'll never forgive you,' I said, 'for doing this to me.'

He got out the map and he said, 'Well, we can't go back. We've got to go on. It isn't very far now. We've just got to go up that bank and then we'll be all right.'

We went up that bank and then I died another death because dropping straight down from the edge of the car was this great, great fall and it was studded with trees. I later used that in *The Mallen Streak*, where one brother murders the other by throwing him down this hill.

'All I remember next was Tom saying, "It's all right now, it's all right. We're on a flat part. There's nothing to fear at all."'

All I remember next was Tom saying, 'It's all right now, it's all right. We're on a flat part. There's nothing to fear at all. It's all flat.' He stopped the car and I got out and again sat on the footboard. There was nothing surrounding us for miles except about twenty yards from the road there stood the wreck of an old house. I understood, after, it had once been an inn where the men driving the horses over Shap Fell stopped and rested and had a drink. But now it only showed a broken roof, a door hanging on its hinges. The walls were standing, but the window frames and every piece of wood seemed to have been stripped from it. I stared at it and the sight of it fell into my subconscious and lay there working until I thought up the story of *The Mallen Streak* and this dirty filthy wreck of a house was to become the setting for the birthplace of a child between two of the main characters in the book. There were many characters in the book, but these two were important. This is where they were trying to shelter from a terrible storm with their horses and it was here

they expressed their love for each other (which was a dangerous thing as the girl was engaged to her lover's half-brother). I described the house, the filthy condition and their coming together, all as I had thought it up on the day of terror on the fells of Northumberland.

Looking out over Alston Moor at dusk.

2 FROM MUCK TO MILLIONS

From the banks of the Tyne came the first railway, an enterprise which created industrial revolution across the world. In Britain, by 1850, a network of railways was established, to be amalgamated in 1854 as The North Eastern Railway.

Since the beginning of the 1840s when the railways had come into existence the North had known a growing prosperity; villages, like Jarrow, through its steel works, had mushroomed into towns. Middlesborough, only a few miles away, had in 1830 been a hamlet housing just over a hundred people but by the year 1853 it was a thriving port with nearly twenty thousand inhabitants. Names had become synonymous with places. Henry Bolckow of Middlesborough who was actually a German by birth; Stephenson of Newcastle; the Lehmans of Sheffield; and not forgetting John Brown, who from an apprentice in a cutlery firm rose to be the owner of a large steel works; Vickers, Armstrong, and Ramsden were names that spelt steel, names upon which thousands upon thousands of men depended for their livelihood; names that were carved in stone at the base of statues and busts, representing the gratitude of thriving towns to the benefactors who had erected gigantic buildings or who had donated a public bath or perhaps a library.

The North at this period was an empire, an empire of coal mines, steel works, and railways, not forgetting glassworks. It was a time when a few outstanding men rose from muck to millions and having done so housed their families in palatial establishments. A percentage of lesser men made a good deal of money and they, too, lived well. And then there was the gentry, and they, as they had always done, lived high.

The Glass Virgin

Coal was the single most significant area of industrial growth in the first part of the nineteenth century and the most important in the way that it encouraged the growth of other industries. It provided the fuel, and other industries returned the favour in their own way.

Left and right: Dunstan coal staithes in Newcastle, well-preserved relic of a once proud industry and reckoned to be the largest wood structure in Europe. The old loading bays can be clearly seen, right.

Right: Looking out from Dunstan coal staithes, the undisturbed view in stark contrast to the busy scene in times past, recalled by Emma in The Whip: *'As she stood on the bank and looked at the different kinds of ships, forming a panorama that stretched away along both banks and made up of scullers, keel boats, barges, small sailing vessels, and large ones that looked gigantic to her eyes, she had been speechless.'*

'Do you remember, Kate, the glow that used to come over Jarrow when the blast furnaces tipped at night.' Kate Hannigan

Coal provided the fuel and the other industries returned the favour in their own way: the railways by decreasing the cost of moving coal; iron and steel by shaping the boats that carried it; glass by utilising unsaleable grades of it, the chemical industry by utilising brine, a pit by-product.

Above: Puddlers at the puddling furnace in which scrap iron would be prepared for the steam hammer to work it free of impurities.

Left: Shinglers working up wrought iron; the steam hammer had been invented in 1851.

The railways encouraged the coal industry by decreasing the cost of moving coal to the ports; the iron and steel industry by shaping the ships that carried the coal to foreign lands; glass by its ability to employ otherwise unsaleable coal; the chemical industry by its use of brine (a nuisance in the pit but invaluable in the manufacture of alkali.) In its turn the chemical industry provided essential ingredients for the glass, pottery, paper, soap, and textile industries.

Coal was thus at the basis of a network of interrelated industries, and the glory of the North Eastern Coalfield was that between 1850 and 1914, either directly or indirectly, it provided vital energy for the urbanisation and industrialisation of Western Europe.

The River

On some days in the early nineteenth century you might see a few hundred sail in the harbour at Shields, where the main collier fleet would lie. And by 1848 there were thirty-six shipbuilding yards along the banks of the Tyne, though none were very large: small

Nineteenth-century hustle and bustle in the crowded moorings of South Shields harbour.

wooden ships, little complex equipment, small work forces – 'mostly scum down there' was Janie's opinion when Rory (the gambling man), with his brother Jimmy, shows his fiancée the boatyard he is about to buy:

Boat building was a good business when the Tyne was gateway to world export markets, but success, was far from assured: 'Takes some grit and guts to start on your own along this stretch.'
The Gambling Man

All the while she kept looking from one to the other of them, but they remained smilingly silent. Then she burst out, 'But the money! You've got the money to buy *this*?' Flinging both arms wide as with joy she gazed about the long room.

'Well – ' Rory pursed his lips – 'enough, enough to put down as a deposit.'

'He didn't get in till six this mornin'.' Jimmy was nodding up at her, and

Above: The waterfront, 1900, with its marine stores, shipsmiths and pump manufacturers.

she turned to Rory and said, 'Gamin'?'

'Yes. Yes, Miss Waggett, that's what they call it, gamin'.'

'And you won?'

'I wouldn't be here showing you this else.'

'How much?'

'Aw well' – he looked away to the side – 'almost eleven pounds at the beginning, but' – he gnawed on his lip for a moment – 'I couldn't manage to get away then, I had to stay on and play. But I was six up anyway when I left.'

Supported by the shipbuilding industry and seafaring traders were a whole host of secondary industries including rope-makers, biscuit-makers, fish curers and, under some threat with the advent of steam, the sail-makers pictured here.

Small South Shields boatyards, then and now, 'woodyards, repair shops, an' things like that.'

'Six pounds?'

'Aye, six pounds.'

'And this place is costin' thirty-five?'

'Aye. But five pounds'll act as a starter. Jimmy's goin' to get the address of the son and I'll write to him the morrow.'

There was a silence between them for a moment until Rory, looking at Janie's profile, said 'What is it?'

'The waterfront, it's ... it's mostly scum down here.'

'Not this end.'

She turned to Jimmy, 'No?'

'No, they're respectable businesses. You know, woodyards, repair shops, an' things like that. An' there's very few live above the shops. There's nobody on yon side of us, an' just that bit of rough land on the other. Eeh!' he laughed, 'I'm sayin' us, as if we had it already ...'

'What do you think?' Rory was gazing at her.

'Eeh!' She walked the length of the room, put her hand out and touched the chest of drawers, then the brass hinges on the oak chest, then the table, and lastly the rocking chair, and her eyes bright, she looked from one to the other and said, 'Eeh! it's amazing. You would never think from the outside it could be like this 'cos it looks ramshackle. But it's lovely, homely.'

'Look in t'other room.' She went into the bedroom, then laughed and said, 'That'll come down for a start.'

She was pointing to the hammock, and Rory answered teasingly, 'No. Why no. Our Jimmy's going to swing in that and we'll lie underneath.'

'Aw you!' Jimmy pushed at the air with his flat hand, then said 'I'll be upstairs, I'll make that grand. Come on, come on up and have a look. Can you manage the ladder?'

Janie managed the ladder, and then she was standing under the sloping

An old staircase leading nowhere, all that is left to remind us of a riverside way of life that has now largely disappeared.

88

Rory's boatyard in the film of
The Gambling Man.

'"Connor's boatyard? Never knew no Connor's boatyard along here."

"It's a small yard, I understand. Mr Connor has only recently taken the yard over."

"Small yard, taken it over?" The old man rubbed the stubble on his chin and said, "Oh aye, now I heard tell of a young 'un starting up there.'

roof looking from one end of the attic to the other and she exclaimed again, 'Eeh! my! did you ever see so many bits of paper and maps and books and things? There's more books here than there are in the master's cases in his study.'   *The Gambling Man*

In those days the route up river to Newcastle was dangerous. Sandbanks, shelves and nasty projecting points of rock helped make the Tyne a real problem of communication and at times impossible to navigate. It was not unknown for people using the Tyne ferries to take meals with them in case they were stranded, and just west of Newcastle there was an island (King's Meadows), big enough to have sheep on it and to support fairs, before it was dredged away later in the century.

The only magistrates able to exercise authority on the water were the Mayor and Aldermen of Newcastle. For years other Tynesiders had campaigned against the town's monopoly of the Tyne, the state of the river, and the high port dues levied: in the first half of the nineteenth century Newcastle took £1,000,000 in dues. But it was only after the Reform Act of 1832, when Gateshead and North and South Shields were given their own MPs, that voices outside Newcastle began to be influential. From that date, whatever party a politician belonged to, he had no chance of being elected in these towns unless abolition of Newcastle's monopoly was part of his manifesto. Finally, in 1850, authority was transferred to the Tyne Improvement Commission, a body which transformed the Tyne in the second part of the century and gave industry a doorway to fast developing export markets.

The Tyne at Newcastle
*– 'sometime doorway to fast
developing export markets'. The
bridges over the Tyne at Newcastle
bear witness to its dramatic
history. Seen here, looking down-
river in the direction of Jarrow and
South Shields, is Robert
Stephenson's High Level (road-
rail) Bridge. Robert was the son of
George Stephenson, inventor of the
first successful steam locomotive in
1814. The steam engine invented
earlier by Cornishman Richard
Trevithick became a locomotive in
1804, but Stephenson's led to the
first passenger line – between
Stockton and Darlington – in
1825. His son Robert's spectacular
bridge, 112 feet above the Tyne,
opened at the moment (1848) that
the city was gaining supremacy
over the Tyne and joined it to a
rail network that had run hitherto
from Redheugh on the south bank
to Carlisle and had required
passengers from Newcastle first to
take a ferry ride across the river.
Next comes the intriguing Swing
Bridge, the low, reddish brown and
white bridge, a project of industri-
alist Sir William Armstrong in
1876; it still turns on its own axis
to enable ships to pass. Finally,
farthest from view, comes the
famous arched Tyne Bridge, a massive iron construction, clear testa-
ment to Newcastle's industrial
past, built in the 1920s. Behind
camera is the King Edward
Bridge, opened for the North
Eastern Railway Company in the
year of Catherine's birth, 1906.
Further upriver is the New
Redheugh (road) Bridge.*

A mercantile background was a likely breeding ground for commercial skills, though not perhaps for the development of over-scrupulous personalities.

Charles Mark Palmer (right) epitomised the interdependent nature of the industrial revolution. His shipyard was responsible for building the first successful iron collier – the John Bowes, but it was his secondary involvement in coal through his directorship of the John Bowes Partnership that enabled him to benefit from easy access to economical quantities of fuel for his ships and his blast furnaces, as well as providing him with direct profits from shipping Bowes coal to London.

'It had been stimulating just to be in Palmer's company... There was enthusiasm, drive and the Midas touch if ever he saw it. Palmer was no age yet, only thirty-eight, and the yard had only been going nine years, but he was coining money, making it hand over fist; not only was he building ships but he was making the materials on the spot to build ships. Jarrow was booming. He had turned it from a village into a literal iron and steel gold mine... Oh, he was no fool was Charles Palmer, this fast-rising star, who was cunningly making a name as a philanthropist. We could all be philanthropists if we could dig gold out of steel.'

George Rosier in *Katie Mulholland*

'They were iron men, steel men; they talked of hardly anything else, for only by iron and steel could they eat. Once a man had worked in Palmer's for some years he felt he would be no good for anything else; nor did he want to be.'
Katie Mulholland

Below: Jarrow, 1900. Charles Palmer virtually called the town into being.

Within a decade of Palmer's success with the launch of the iron-hulled collier, the John Bowes, in 1852, more than ten shipyards on the Tyne were building iron ships and employing more than 4,000 men between them.

By the beginning of the 20th century more than a quarter of the world's tonnage was built in the shipyards of the North East. But the boom was not to last.

The Kingdom of the Blind

Me granda used to say that all pitmen hewed more coal at the corner end, or at their games of quoits, and pitch and toss, than they ever did down the mine. Added to this was my own experience of miners, derived more from the way they treated their wives and families, the females thereof, than from the men themselves.

It wasn't until about 1952 (long after I had moved to Hastings) that my opinion of miners turned a complete somersault.

High above Birtley, where Catherine experienced firsthand 'the kingdom of everlasting night'. The old pithead at Kibblesworth affords this view of an area that once supported a number of mining communities. Close by you will also come across the Ravensworth Arms at Lamesley where Catherine's parents met. Leave Newcastle by way of Team Valley.

All that remains to remind visitors of Birtley's sometime coal mining base is part of the winding gear (the wheel) on display in the town centre.

I was meeting my seven cousins from Birtley for the first time for about twenty-eight years. The four boys had always worked down the pits, and I angered them with my remarks about the price of coal in the South. The result of our verbal battle was that they challenged me to go down the mine. The thought petrified me, but what could I do with those four indignant men facing me. I went down with Peter – he was a deputy at the Betty Pit in Birtley – and was down about three hours. I almost embraced the daylight when I stepped back out of the cage, and from that moment wanted, sincerely and genuinely wanted to pin medals on every pitman. The outcome of my nerve wracking experience was my fourth novel, *Maggie Rowan*. Maggie has challenged Ann to go down the pit in order to face up to her irrational fear for David's safety:

As they dropped into the earth, the light from their lamps showed the rough-hewn surface of the walls not more than inches from the sides of the cage. The movement was slow, almost gentle, and in no way to be compared with the drop she had heard men speak of. And when with a slight bump the cage reached the bottom her terror for a moment was stilled; only to return with sickening force when she stepped out in to the 'road'.

The road. How often she had heard her father speak of the road, when unconsciously she had created her own picture of it: a broad road, leading from a kind of hallway in which the cage landed; the road might narrow later on and men might have to crawl, but at its beginning the road was broad and high. But now she was standing in it, and it was little broader than a passage, about ten

In the 19th century, the mines were the real hell. The picture (right) is from the film of the 1971 novel, The Dwelling Place. *The Brodie children are the focus of the story which is most striking for its deep cut into the hopelessness and exploitation of the poor. Their mother was rescued from a coal pit in the West Riding when she was only 12.*

feet wide at most and seeming to be filled with a row of small trucks, which stretched away into the blackness and were lost.

She raised her eyes to the roof, about three feet above her head, and could scarcely believe what she saw: criss-crossed pieces of wood holding up huge boulders of rock, and these pieces of wood kept in place by pit props – just pit props – seeming to form a straight wall to the passage as they disappeared in the distance; and behind them lay masses of loose rock, not coal as she had surmised, but rock.

She moved away in the wake of the others; and her attention was suddenly taken from herself, for, to avoid stepping into pools of water, she had to keep her lamp playing continually around her feet.

They were walking single file in no more than a breadth of three feet, for the coal tracks overhanging the track took up most of the room. But once past the end of the trucks the ground became fairly even and the deputy's voice came to her as if he was speaking through a funnel, saying, 'We'll turn off here for a minute and see the ponies.'

She stopped. Oh no; that was one thing she couldn't do, she couldn't bear

to see the ponies. She would let them go on. But this escape was denied her for a man coming up behind said, 'You'd better not dawdle, lass; you'd better tag along. What are you trying to do, get lost?'

'No. They're looking at the ponies: I don't want to go in.'

He brought his blackened face down to hers in genuine surprise. 'Why, miss? Why not for? They'd like to see you, they don't often see a lass.'

He took her arm, determined to prove his point, and led her off the main road and along a passage. And she saw the ponies in their stables.

They looked fat and well-kept; but oh, the poor things! Down here all their lives, after having known the freedom of running wild. Oh, it was awful. Never to see the light of day again!

Ann walked silently past the man who had brought her in, and this time he made no effort to impose his will on her. She stood at the corner of the passage adjoining the roadway, and words of her father talking to Tom came back to her: 'Stick to your pony, lad, and it's ten to one you'll escape half the accidents; the pony knows what's afoot minutes afore you do. It's a sixth sense they have. Many's the life that's been saved by a pony.'

Yes; but to keep them down here all the time. Oh, dear God! She looked

'She was walking into a world that didn't belong to any kind of life she had yet imagined. She was going along what appeared to be a tunnel with iron rails down the middle, and she went to step in between them for easier walking when Kate with a bawl that nearly took her head off cried, "Do you want to be run over afore you start? Don't be so bloody gormless, lass, that's the rolley way. Look." She pointed ahead to where a young lad was coming towards them leading a horse, and as they came nearer, Tilly could see the three bogies full of coal rattling behind the horse.' Tilly Trotter

102

Above: from the film of Tilly Trotter. *Coal provided the fuel of industrial revolution, and conditions were often appalling. In the 1830s, when we first meet Tilly, George Rosier is the manager of the Sopwith mine and it isn't only ponies but women and children who are the forlorn subjects of 'the coal kingdom,' as Catherine referred to it in another novel –* Our John Willie: *'Aye, the kingdom of slaves, the kingdom of the blind, the kingdom of long everlasting night.'*

about her, but her eyes could travel no distance at all before being checked by stones or props. And not only the ponies, but Davie and all those men spent half their lives in this place, and in others like it; and were really terrified, too, of being stood off – so many pits were idle. Yet she wished at this moment from the bottom of her heart that the Venus, and this one too, were idle, for then her Davie would be up above, and he'd get another job somehow. Yet this she knew was a vain hope; he'd always go back to the pit; his dream was of the day when they'd get extra shifts in and earn some more money to make living a little easier ... It wasn't right somehow.

The deputy was now pointing out the pit props, which were no longer brown but white; and this was nothing, he was saying, to what they would see when they got into the mothergate. There, fungi as big as their hands grew on the props.

Ann ceased to listen to the deputy's voice, nor was she interested in those things which were apparently peculiar to this mine, she was weighed down by

the overpowering terribleness of it all; but when the party again stopped and the deputy suggested that to see just how dark the mine was they should cover up their lamps, a protest escaped her and she cried, 'Eeh, no'; whereupon Maggie took the lamp from her hand and within a few minutes they were standing in darkness, the like of which she had never imagined possible – thick, heavy, clinging darkness, that hurt the eyeballs, that became alive and pressed on you.

'Don't speak for a minute,' said the deputy.

Now silence was added ... the darkness and silence of the eternity of the damned. It flashed through Ann's brain that the roaring flames of hell would be preferable to this, for in hell there would be sound and colour; here there was

'This one should have been condemned years ago; but no, no, they wanted their last drop of blood. The whole country's riddled with pits now.' Our John Willie

The leather straps across the man's shirt kept in place a pad that protected his back when 'righting' waggons that had come off the tracks: a strenuous job, but judging by the size of his wrists, one that he was equal to.

nothing yet everything, everything that was needed to bring the dark terrors of the soul to the surface.

'Oh no!' Her own suppressed scream added to her terror. And as the lamps twinkled again, their small lights appearing brilliant in contrast to the blackness, she wanted to be sick. She turned to Maggie to make yet another protest, but her words and supplicating outstretched hand were checked, for

hanging loose and saliva was running over her lower lip.

'You'll get out; come on. Only go steady, else you'll likely as not break your legs, and then you'll be in a worse fix. You should never have come down. Hadn't you any idea what it would be like?'

'Yes... no. Well, not like this. I want to get out.'

'There now, take it easy. You see, you are in the main road now and it won't be long.'

They passed an old man, a solitary figure, standing as if he was part of the inanimate depth wherein he worked.

Without preliminary explanation the deputy said, 'She shouldn't have come down,' and the old man answered 'No, God fits the nerve to the need.'

As the cage moved upwards the light from above grew stronger, and she peered at the walls of the shaft, gathering to herself the rays of light... Oh, to be out in the light and the sun! The sun. To see the sun again. How many aeons of time had passed since she saw the sun!... and David. He didn't see the sun or light for over seven hours of each day, and then in the winter when he came up it was dark... Darkness. For days and days, darkness. Oh, David!

The cage bumped to a standstill, and with Bert's hand on her arm she stepped out on to the platform, and right to the feet of David!

Maggie Rowan

The Cost

The cost of industrial expansion was measured in the employment conditions and the lives of the men, women and children these industrialists employed.

The most dangerous period for miners was in the nineteenth century when colliers were mining deep pits in areas where they had no real knowledge of the level of danger from water or gas. As the size of shifts increased, numbers of dead would be measured in hundreds from a single incident. The situation came to a head in 1862 with the New Hartley disaster in which more than two hundred men and boys were killed.

When I was researching *The Menagerie* I wrote to the Ministry of Mines. They sent me white papers, huge maps depicting everything that had happened after an explosion. They were a fearful sight: even a man's bait tin or the exact site where another man's head was blown off, were pinpointed. I worked *The Menagerie* from these records:

The town was still, the shops were closed, and no traffic moved on the main road. The day had started quietly and the quietness had grown with each hour. When people stirred they did so softly; when they spoke, their words, broad as they might be, did not rise with the sing-song intonation and fill the air, but hovered close about them as if loath to jar this day of sorrows. The funeral

Principal among local mining disasters were those at the Stanley pit in 1909, in which 168 people died (the stark picture, above right, shows the removal of the bodies), and at New Hartley in 1862 where there had been one shaft for all purposes – men, coal and ventilation – making rescue impossible. When finally the rescuers reached their destination, they discovered notes written by the men, describing the scene as it had been before they died, describing the prayer meetings that had taken place towards the end.

For those fortunate to have survived disaster, the experience left its mark: 'From that time William had suffered from nightmares, nightmares in which he was suffocating among mangled bodies and blood.' Katie Mulholland

Below right: The funeral cortege following the Stanley pit disaster: 'The funeral route was black with people; and as the long line of hearses moved slowly to the cemetery, women cried, men cried, and small children were unusually silent.' The Menagerie

route was black with people; and as the long line of hearses moved slowly to the cemetery, women cried, men cried, and small children were unusually silent.

A group of rescuers at the Stanley pit disaster.

    Larry was the only representative of his family. The one uncle and three cousins he had were scattered over the country. The uncle was confined to his bed, and the cousins for varying reasons could not attend. Cables bearing frantic messages had come from Australia, but no one expected anyone from there. Neighbours and friends flanked him, but seemingly he was alone. Of his father and Jack, he did not think 'I am walking with them for the last time' because for days now they had been strangely nearer to him than ever they had been when alive. Some part of each of them had burrowed into his being; he felt he was no longer one but three men. But he would recognise the responsibilities of two only, his own, and his father's. His mother was his responsibility; so was Aunt Lot; but Jack's child... Here his particular self was constantly proving the point against Jack's pleading. The child was Lena's; she should be found and made to take it. Yet within himself he knew that Lena had gone for good, and that what was finally to become of the child would rest with him. And at the moment these three people represented his world, and their combined pressure lay on his shoulders like a roof fall.

The cemetery lay on a rising fell on the outskirts of the town, and from any part of it could be seen the shafts of the two pits. As the heart-breaking service went on, and names were called and the coffins lowered, and flowers sprinkled and muffled sobs and moans filled the air, heads would be lifted to the pit wheels, and like monster eyes in which was reflected nothing but indifference the wheels stared back and seemed to say, 'You asked for it. Who started me anyway? You want coal and more coal. You must pay for it.'

Frank and Jack were laid side by side, and as Larry stepped blindly back from the grave, he too seemed forced to raise his eyes over the mass of heads. The wheels looked at him. First the Venus then the Phoenix, and at the sight of them he yelled in his head, 'Damn you! Blast you!'

A woman near him quietly fainted, sliding down between two relatives as if she had just decided to sit, while another, unable to control her sobs, verged on hysteria. A man, whose son had just been lowered, gave a cry like a wounded animal and, turning from the grave, his hand shielding his face, he pushed his way aggressively through the crowd.

At last it was over, the dead were left in the bower of flowers. And it was of the flowers that Larry was thinking as he walked out of the gates. Never in his life did he want to see or smell another flower. Always would he be reminded of that grave when he saw a bunch of flowers. The smell of them was strong in his nostrils now and filling his head with a sick ache. He felt their scent would remain round him for ever.

The Menagerie

Recession, Depression and Collapse

Quite suddenly on a May day in 1866 the empire of the North shuddered and collapsed as if struck by an earthquake, and small men, middle men and those in high places felt the tremors.

There was panic in the City of London. Banks failed; railways went out of business; steel companies had to join forces in order to survive; businesses that had been held jealously within families were either bankrupt or were merged with companies that had been fortunate enough to escape the earthquake.

This one and that were blamed for the disaster but the fault seemed to be with the company of Overand and Gurney, who financed a great deal of the Northern industries at the time, and were overspent by many millions; and so the flame of panic spread from the banking houses in London and swept the North.

The Glass Virgin

Gurneys were part of a great Quaker group which had built up enormous financial business in the course of the nineteenth century.

With collapse came poverty and queues for the soup kitchen, here at the poor house in Newcastle. Today the building stands eerily empty on the edge of the huge roundabout on the north side of the Tyne bridge.

1934, the dismantling of the huge cranes at Palmer's.

'Yet what echo do I hear?
Palmer's of Hebburn
Is to close.
Is this the prelude
To fear
Resurrecting the
Slump
That was never to return?'

the yard – hit me personally.' She slanted her eyes at him, and there was a shyness in her look as she said, 'You see, it stopped my wedding. Peter losing his savings, all twelve hundred pounds of it, and being responsible for his mother and the house; his father's dead. Then the fact that if we married I would lose my job...'

'How's that?'

'Oh, they don't allow you to teach after you are married, not the women. We, too, are dead if we marry. But I suppose it's to be expected. There aren't enough jobs for the male teachers. We know a friend of ours who put in for a post down South; he's a maths master. Do you know how many applicants there were for the job? Two hundred and fifty.'

'You don't say!' His brows were drawn together. Then he said 'Your fiancé – he... didn't get any of his money back from the firm?'

'As long as you could see the cranes you felt that your job was secure' had become a saying of the past. Few who lived through the 1930s on Tyneside cared to dwell on the experience. Today's mighty cranes (above) maintain something of the aura of long ago, but the culture of Tyneside is now based elsewhere.

'No, but he was just like hundreds of others in the town. There were families who had saved and saved for years and put it into Palmer's; perhaps it was only a couple of hundred pounds or so, but to them it was a fortune, and they lost every penny, and now they're on the dole and stunned by the hopelessness of it all.'

He looked hard at her as she looked at the gigantic wreck, and he had the strange disturbing urge to grab her by the hand and run pell-mell from this place. He had a picture of them tearing down the main street never stopping until they reached an open space where they could see nothing of tangled iron, dreary grey streets and hopeless-looking men and women.

'Come,' he said, his voice brisk-sounding. 'Let's get out of this.'

Katie Mulholland

The key factor in the story of industrial growth proved to be the export boom and the lack of foreign competition. Once the rest of Europe began to catch us up and undercut our production prices, the end was in sight. Weak companies found no support from the government in the form of subsidies or tariffs on imports – none

A solitary tug on the river today. In days gone by there would have been hundreds plying the Tyne.

when the Belgian glass industry threatened; German chemical industry came through... and no one felt the effects of the government's resolute non-protectionist policy more than the workers.

In fact even when the spiral of industrial growth was in its ascendancy there had been eddies in the opposite direction, depressions which resulted in large numbers of unemployed. And besides unemployment there was the problem of *under*-employment, which often left people worse off than being on the dole. Today dockers have a substantial minimum wage to sign on, but until the decasualisation of the docks they were paid by the shift. How many shifts in a week was completely unpredictable, for while the regular steamship traffic could be forecast fairly accurately, there was an enormous amount of ship traffic coming in and out of the Tyne which could not be. To service it required a pool of labour hanging about the docks and not getting paid.

The cancer of unemployment was eating the country, and the Tyneside in particular. It was eating into initiative and hope, and doubling despair. A man,

NOSTALGIA

Oh would the North were as it was
When I was little Katie
When ships were born from
Palmer's womb
And slag lit scarlet and black the
*   night sky*
And rivets flew like sparks from
*   stars*
And men were proud to work and
*   sweat.*
And yet?
This is just reminiscing talk
No – I would not have the North
As it was
When I was little Katie
For then no workman owned a car
Or took a holiday across the sea
Nor dare he stand and say to them
'Lad, I'm as good as thee.'

Oh, little Katie of long ago
Of long, long ago.

Tyneside images of collapse, like this mangled dry dock gate close to the site of Palmer's, seem to hold the hour.

becoming unemployed, went on the dole; and he would sign on each day before vainly doing the round of the shipyards. And in the evening he would stand at the corner with his pals, who were in the same predicament as himself, and they would hide their feelings in jokes. If he lay in bed at night and wondered what was to become of him and the wife and bairns once the dole was finished, he gave little sign of it during the day.

It is said that man can get used to any condition if he is in it long enough, and it would seem there was truth in this, for, as the years went on and the dole bred the Means Test, most of the men on the Tyne had forgotten how it felt to carry a bait tin – in fact they doubted whether there had ever been a time in their lives when they had worked. The younger men didn't have to wonder

Warehouses lie empty, the Customs House at South Shields (see below) has long since ceased to matter.

about this; those born just prior to or during the 1914 war never knew what it was to be employed. Even those apprenticed to the few small firms still in existence were stood off immediately they reached the age of nineteen.

It was strange, too, how stark poverty changed the flavour of the jokes from sex to food.

'Well, I'm off for me dinner.'

'What's it the day, lad?'

'Chicken.'

'Chicken agin?'

'Aye... I'm so bloody full of chicken I've got the urge to gan an' sit on a clutch of eggs.'

And so it went on. Here and there a man suddenly ended the struggle, and the effect on his mates, oddly enough, was such as to stiffen their fibre. 'It's no use taking things like that,' would be their attitude; 'things can't get any worse; the bloody Government will have to do something if they don't want trouble. Hang on a bit longer.'

Colour Blind

Palmer's Tavern, hard by the yard, seems fated to remind us of this numbing era when promise ended in despair.

End of the Road

During one period of great depression – this was when my mother was a child – me granda worked in the workhouse, breaking stones at a shilling a day. The shilling was paid as a voucher which had to be taken to a grocery shop, and if anyone dared to ask the shop-keeper to put in a penn'orth of baccy he was likely to lose the voucher altogether. The utter degradation of the workhouse is described in *Our John Willie*:

'Come on.' He tugged John Willie into step with him, and it was only when, half an hour later, he came within sight of the workhouse walls that he stopped, and the effect of what he was about to do overwhelmed him.

Slowly he dropped on to his hunkers, and now in elaborate sign language he explained. Pointing first to the formidable grey buildings, he then pushed his finger into the young boy's chest, after which he placed the flat of his hand on his own breast, bowed his head, then rose to his feet and did a standing march.

John Willie understood, he understood only too well. His eyes screwed up, his mouth opened wide and from it was tumbled a rapid succession of 'Huhs' that grew louder in protest.

'Look! Look!' Davy rose to his feet and taking John Willie by the shoulders shook him as he cried, 'Listen. Listen.' He always said listen, even when he knew it was a silly thing to say.

John Willie now became quiet, still. His mouth closed, his eyes stretched wide, there was no movement in any part of his thin body while he stared into Davy's troubled face.

Unemployed men, stripped of their dignity, make toys.

'I've got to go... to find work.' Davy now demonstrated digging with a shovel. After this he pointed in the direction opposite to the workhouse, then counting on his fingers, 'One, two, three, four, five,' for that was one thing he could do, he could count up to twenty, he brought his arm in a wide circling movement, finishing up by once more placing his finger on John Willie's chest. And although John Willie made no signs whatever, Davy knew that his brother was aware of what lay in front of him.

Slowly now they went towards the gates. When he rattled the chain a man came out of the lodge and, looking through the bars, said, 'Aye, what you after?'

'I've got a ticket for bread.'

'Another one of 'em!'

The porter took a key that was hanging from his belt and unlocked the chain and pulled open the gates, and they went inside, John Willie walking so close to Davy's side that he almost impeded his movements.

'Go along there to the clerk, he'll see to you.' The man pointed into the distance, and they went towards a door, then through it and into a bare flag-stoned corridor. There were windows on one side of the corridor and through them he looked on to a big yard that was walled on all sides by high buildings. The yard was full of people, men, women, and children, and they were all doing odd things. Some were standing with their faces to the walls, some were

126

'The town looked dead, it even smelt dead to him. The district around the station had appeared dreary enough, but these dejected grey streets with groups of men leaning against end walls, all attired in similar uniform, cap, muffler, and greasy-looking oddments of suits, were depressing to say the least.' Katie Mulholland

jumping up and down as if skipping but without ropes; others were laughing. But there was one woman near the window almost within arm's length of him who had her face turned up to the sky and the tears were washing her cheeks. Then there was the noise. It was chattering noise, a mixture of all kinds of noises like that made by birds in a cage.

'They're the dafties.'

He swung round startled to look up at a big gangling woman who had a wooden bucket in one hand and a scrubbing brush and dirty cloth in the other, and she nodded her head towards the window as she grinned widely, saying, 'They're all daft, barmy. I'm not daft. I'm Emma Steel, and I'm not daft.' At

Harton workhouse, where Catherine worked in the laundry. The asylum was to the right. The stone-breaking yard was at the back where her grandfather broke stones for a shilling a day.

'But God was good, and had showered his special blessing over them, when all around, weeping women and grim-faced men had watched their last sticks of furniture being carried out by the bums before wending their heart-breaking way down the Jarrow Road to East Jarrow, through Tyne Dock and down Stanhope Road, to where Talbot Road showed the grim gates at the far end, which, once entered, a family was no longer a family but merely segregated individuals with numbers on each of their garments.' Colour Blind

this she turned and walked away to the end of the corridor where, putting the bucket on the ground, she knelt down by it and started to scrub the stones.

It was seconds before Davy realised that he was still staring at her, his mouth slightly agape. She said she wasn't daft, well, she wasn't among that lot but he had never seen anybody look dafter.

'What do you want?'

He swung round in the other direction now and looked at a woman in a kind of uniform dress with a starched cap on her head. The woman scrubbing the corridor had a cap on her head too but it was a different one; and all those

Harton Workhouse is now South Tyneside Hospital. The spire has gone, as have the old asylum buildings and of course the stone-breaking yard at the rear, but you cannot fail to recall its sorry history. The workhouse was a fearful presence in the lives of the poor. Fear of it, like fear of the Church, had strong historical roots.

women out in the yard, they were wearing caps, like bonnets, dirty white bonnets.

'I've got a ticket' – he held out the slip – 'for bread from...Parson Murray.'

'Go in the end door.'

'Ta.' He nodded at the woman as she walked away, and it was some seconds still before he could make his feet move towards the door at the end of the corridor.

When he opened the door he found he was looking into a room where four men were seated at high desks, and all were writing rapidly. The one nearest the door lifted his head and stared from Davy to John Willie, then back to Davy before saying, 'Aye, what is it?'

Davy repeated that he had a ticket for bread and held it out. The man looked at the slip of paper. Then raising his head and looking from one to the other again, he said, 'For the two of you?'

'Yes, sir.'

Left: The laundry at Harton Workhouse. Catherine worked there from October 22, 1924. 'The checker whose position I filled is the furthest left of the four women wearing Sunday uniforms; the other three – left to right – are the assistant head, the manageress, and a seamstress. The girls without caps are paid hands (see how happy they are?); the rest are inmates. Once a woman got her hand entwined in a sheet and dragged on to the hot steel bed, before being crushed by the rollers that can be seen behind.'

Later, on part duty in the evenings, Catherine was in charge of admissions – 'the men to one side, the women to the other, the children to the nurses' home or the nursery, or an old couple, knowing they'd have to spend the rest of their lives in the workhouse. Shields Workhouse in those days was not far removed from the Dickensian era.'

'You'll have to do four hours stone breaking you know.'

'Yes, sir.'

'I can't see him breaking many stones.'

'I... I can do enough for us both.'

'No, no, it doesn't work like that; a man can only work to his full capacity, as can a boy. You are expected to give full capacity in return for your food.'

'I'll work extra hard, sir.'

The man was looking at John Willie. 'What is the matter with him? He's puny. How old is he?'

'Ten, sir. He's... he's deaf and dumb, sir.'

'Deaf and dumb? Ten?' The man gave a little shake of his head as if he didn't believe it, then added, not unkindly, 'If you work all day you can have a mid-day meal.'

'If... if you don't mind, sir, I'll... I'll just take the bread.'

There was rising in Davy a desperate urge to be away from this place.

The man now took a metal disc from a drawer and, handing it to Davy,

3 MY AIN FOLK

I was born when Kate was twenty-four and the life she was made to endure because of me would have driven anyone less strong not only to drink but into the madhouse. The cruelty of the bigoted poor has to be witnessed to be believed. It has to be lived with to be understood.

When my mother, sick to the depths of her soul, as I know now she was, had to come home from 'her place' (my mother's first spell of service was for a butcher in Stanhope Road) and say she was going to have a baby, The Fathar, as he was always called, was for killing her.

Our Kate, aged about forty, standing at the back of Number Ten. 'Kate's troubles hung over her head like an avalanche about to plunge down and bury her.'

Kate had committed the unforgivable sin, yet when I was born and she had milk fever and her breasts swelled to bursting, the fathar was supposed to have saved her life by sucking the milk from them. It seems incredible to me that she should have looked upon

137

this act as something almost heroic for, remembering him as I do, I can see that he would have enjoyed this operation – he was a frustrated, licentious man. His antidote against this, which the ailing health of me grandma could not alleviate, was drink and a dirty tongue, which he used against all women. Yet I must say that only on rare occasions did he let himself go in my presence, at least when he was sober. I feel grateful to him for this, for he had been known to make even the toughest women in the New Buildings blush.

As the years went on I think that of the two, me grandma was harder on Kate than the fathar, because, when coming home from place on her rare days off, if she'd attempt to take me in her arms me grandma would grab me from her, rearrange my clothes and almost dust me down as if Kate's hands had contaminated me in some way.

At the time she met my father she was working in an inn in Lamesley. She was working in the bar, and had been for two or three years. Her sister, Mary, who was three years younger, was a housemaid, and a very haughty, hot-tempered housemaid at that. I am not quite sure of the name of the owners of the inn at that time but I do

The inn at Lamesley where Kate worked behind the bar and met Catherine's father; it features in her novel, The Moth: *'In the inn at Lamesley he had met an old gaffer and paid for the history of the district in two half-pints of ale.'*

138

Today The Ravensworth Arms, as the inn is called, is as accommodating as ever. Within easy reach of Newcastle, south along Team Valley, you can still sup in the saloon bar where Catherine's parents first met.

know that the daughter was Miss Jenny. Kate often spoke of her. Also of the pitmen who used to take the long trek past the inn to the mine, and on pay day, which was once a fortnight, have a blow up in the bar and a pay up for the odd pints that had gone on the slate. She must have been a favourite with them, for she was an attractive woman in those days, gay, warm, large-hearted.

My father, I understand, first set eyes on her when she served him in the saloon.

Kate never told me anything about him until six years before she died. It was my Aunt Mary who, when I was sixteen, gave me the sketchy outline of my beginnings and set up in my mind an inordinate pride, a sense of false superiority and a burning desire to meet this wonderful creature who had shocked me into being. This man. This gentleman. Oh, yes, he was a gentleman. My Aunt Mary stated this with emphasis. She had no love for her sister, Kate. Later in life when Kate became the object of her scorn, she still remained jealous of her, for people liked Kate, loved her in spite of everything. Mary did not have a nature that one could love, and when she imparted this news to me it was to hurt Kate, make me more ashamed of her. Yet deep in me I knew that my Aunt Mary wasn't a patch on our Kate. But Mary was often kind to me, it was only her scorn of Kate that made me dislike her. Anyway, Mary said this gentleman went head over heels as soon as he saw Kate.

What did this gentleman do for a living?

Nobody has ever been able to tell me.

How did Mary know he was a gentleman?

Well, he wore a black coat with an astrakhan collar. He had a high hat and carried a silver mounted walking stick and black kid gloves, like 'The Silver King', she said. 'And he spoke different... lovely.'

For two years the gentleman courted Kate. He did not come regularly but when he did he took her out, arranging his visits to her day off. She looked at no one else in the way she did at him. She was deeply in love. What did she expect from this association? She never said. But, knowing her level-headedness, I feel that she knew from the beginning that it was hopeless and therefore she kept him in his place, except for once; and once was enough. It seems pitiable to me at this distance that it wasn't until she was twenty-three that she first went with a man. I say first; it was the one and only time she had this kind of association with my father, and it's more pitiable still that she never had this association with anyone else until over sixteen years later when she married David McDermott, because she was of a loving nature. I can feel myself getting angry when I think that she was branded as a fallen woman – and you needed to make a mistake only once and give evidence of it in order to acquire this prefix in those days – while today girls still at the school indulge in intimacy for kicks. If I hadn't stopped believing in God this injustice would surely have acted as a springboard against believing in a benevolent father, a controller of destinies, someone who has our welfare at heart, for such a deity must surely have had his favourites, and Kate wasn't one of them.

My bitterness is not for myself because I realise now that in being part of 'the gentleman' – and I have my tongue in my cheek even as I write the word – I have a great deal to be thankful for, for he provided the norm at which I aimed. It was him in me that pushed and pulled me out of the drabness of my early existence.

Big Houses Peopled by Ladies and Gentlemen

One day when I was five, and walking through the arches from the Docks – from a very small child I was used to going about on my own – I saw someone coming towards me who apparently I didn't want to meet for I crossed over the road and, turning my face to the blank,

Highfield Manor in the film of Tilly Trotter. *'Perhaps I owe my descriptions of big country houses to the gentleman in me, "the other half" which knew just what was needed.'*

black wall, walked sideways until I had passed them, for I knew that if I couldn't see them they couldn't see me. I was to follow this pattern for many years; whenever I didn't want to face up to some reality, I would turn my face to a wall; and always I would see a picture, which became the focal point of my striving, because it presented to me a different way of life. It showed me a big house peopled by ladies and gentlemen, and surrounded by cars, horses and servants. Of course, I was in the picture, dead centre.

The nearest reality to the picture, in the vicinity of East Jarrow, were the villages of Harton and Westoe. Katie Mulholland began, against all odds, to make her fortune in the old part of Shields. Despite wagging tongues she made the transition to Westoe in the best capitalist tradition:

In the fourteen years that had passed since the day Katie became the owner of 12, 13 and 14 Crane Street many changes had taken place in her life, and also in the town. The latter had spread itself far beyond the confines of the river. An 1827 map had shown wide stretches of open land between the town and parishes of Westoe and Harton owned by a certain Mr Cookson, who in 1837 began the manufacture of sheet glass, but with the years Shields had encroached upon this land until now Westoe village, although clinging tenaciously to its aristocratic bearing, was no longer a separate entity but a suburb of Shields.

It is said that the better part of Shields was full of worthy people, but once a man wanted prestige he moved to Westoe or Harton. Here were to be found the owners of shipyards, foundries, glass-works, breweries, coal-mines, quarries, pipe factories, soap factories, candle factories, pottery factories, bankers and property owners.

The really big houses stood back from the roads, guarded by their high stone walls and stiff shrubberies, and titles weren't unknown in this quarter. The not so ostentatious but still grand houses were in rows or terraces, each house being of a different design, some being taller than others, some having porticoes over their front doors, and most having gardens with hedges to screen their lower windows from the public gaze, from strollers who came in from Shields, to walk under the trees and gape at their betters, or watch the gentry riding in their carriages. Trees lined the roads, from which they were separated by white wooden railings, inlet at intervals to make a carriageway to the gates or doors of the superior dwellings.

Here and there you would find a small house called a cottage, which might have six to eight rooms. In 1880 Katie Mulholland, known now to some as Mrs Fraenkel, had bought six so-called cottages and had recently purchased a much larger domain in which she was considering taking up residence. Not that Mrs Fraenkel wanted to move into the heart of the elite, for she had been happy in her present home in Ogle Terrace for the past eight years; and Ogle Terrace, one of the best of the residential quarters in South Shields, had proved test enough to a woman who had made her money by buying tenement houses that lined the river; houses that were known by her name, Katie Mulholland's houses. And by the conduct of the occupants of her houses she had further gained an appendage to her name which was nothing to be proud of, but against which she was powerless to defend herself, for did she not live on the money she received in rents? Moreover, as was whispered in some parlours, did she not live openly with a Swede, and, whisper softly, had she not been in prison through running one of her houses as a place of infamy?   *Katie Mulholland*

In the television series of *The Mallens*, a house in Derbyshire was

Langley Castle, close to Catherine and Tom's sometime home in Langley village, before renovation and conversion to a hotel.

'The boy stared long and hard at the pile upon pile of stone, and when he made no comment his father said, "Well, what d'you think?"

"It's old."

"Aye, lad, it's old."

"And it wants mendin'."

The tall man burst out laughing as he said, "Right again, it wants mendin'."' A Dinner of Herbs

used for High Banks Hall. But none of my big country houses – High Banks, Greenwall, Redford – are based on real buildings. They are all products of the imagination, and perhaps more than a little, part of my 'picture on the wall', the focal point of my striving.

By the age of twenty-seven I had worked and saved sufficiently hard to be able to afford a 15-roomed, former gentleman's residence called The Hurst, and that was years before I began to write, and three years before I met Tom. As a teenager, after a childhood in the cramped conditions of 10 William Black Street, I remember promising myself that I would never marry but would, instead, give myself what the kind of man I should marry would give me: a very nice house with plenty of space.

So perhaps I owe my descriptions of big country houses to the gentleman in me, 'the other half' which knew just what was needed.

Whatever is the case I have no doubt that my houses are realistic, for one day I received a telephone call from a man living in

'The house of my imagination': The Hurst, Hoadswood Road, Hastings, a fifteen-roomed gentleman's residence. The relationship between Catherine and The Hurst lasted twenty-one years. Finally, in 1954, she and Tom gave up the struggle with it – for it was a struggle from the first day the rains came and washed through those roofs – 'it had eaten up my energy and every penny poor Tom and I were earning.'

Scotland who had read one of my books. He was convinced that I had described his house and asked me when I had been there. When I told him that I had only been to Scotland once, on a day trip to Edinburgh when I was twenty-two, he said, 'But you have described my house in great detail, from the kitchen up. Have you seen pictures?' Of course I hadn't, but during our conversation I believe he mentioned only one feature of my description that wasn't quite the same!

The Kitchen at Number Ten

Since returning to Tyneside I have had six houses and redesigned three of them. But of all the rooms I have ever lived in, the kitchen in William Black Street is the most important. Everything that I have written since seems to have been bred in that kitchen. Other things have been bred in me – the niceties, if you like – but the rawness of life came from that kitchen. The kitchen is the heart of the matter, for the kitchen was the axis about which revolved the lives of those nearest to me – my people, be they what they may...

We did not live in number ten when we first went to the New

The kitchen in the film of The Fifteen Streets. '*The kitchen was the hub of my life; it was the centre of the universe from which all pain and pleasure sprang. In it would be enacted battles both physical and mental.*'

Buildings but in an upstairs house further up the street; but we did not live there long. Number ten was a downstairs house and had three rooms. The front room, into which you stepped from a tiny hall-way that allowed only for the opening of the door, held a green plush suite – two stiff-backed armchairs, four single ones and a long couch – an oval table standing on a centre leg and a double brass bed. The bed lay in an alcove and you walked down the side of it to get to the door which led into the kitchen.

How a room the size of our kitchen could hold so much I don't know, for in its centre stood a large kitchen table of the better kind, with a leather covered top. Under the window that looked into the backyard stood another table, an oblong one, which was used for cooking. The fireplace was the old fashioned open black range and on the left of it for many years stood a great ugly unused gas stove. In front of the range was a massive steel fender, four feet long, and a conglomeration of steel fire irons, none standing less than two feet high. On the floor, along the length of the fender was a clippy mat, a great heavy affair that I couldn't lift even when I was fourteen. On this mat stood a high backed wooden chair, 'the fathar's chair', on

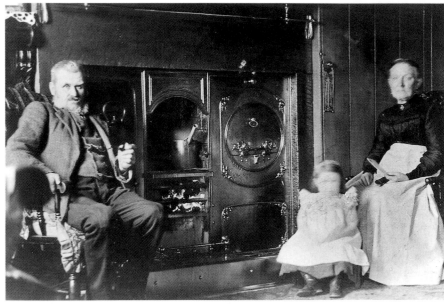

which no one dared to sit but himself. Standing against the wall opposite the door that led out of the kitchen into the scullery was a chest of drawers. A six foot long wooden saddle – like a settee or couch – was set against the wall opposite the fireplace, but to get on to it you had to pull the table out or scramble over the head. Above it hung a picture of Lord Roberts sitting on a horse with a black man standing at his side. For years I believed the rider to be me Granda when he was in India, and when he levelled abuse at the picture, which he often did, I thought he was speaking to the black man.

What we called the scullery held two shelves and a backless chair, on which stood the tin dish used for all purposes that required water. Beyond was the pantry, a narrow slit with one long shelf. The tap was at the bottom of the yard, where also were the two lavatories. In this latter we were fortunate, there being a lavatory to each house. The back door leading to the upstairs house was on the left of our kitchen window, and opposite, running the complete length of the wall from our bedroom window to the coal house doors, were hen crees, always full of hens and ducks.

You reached the door of the bedroom by edging between the oblong table, the kitchen table and the head of the saddle, the bedroom in which I slept with my mother on a flea-ridden feather mattress, against which, with my conscripted assistance, she waged a fruitless war for years.

Why didn't we get rid of the mattress? What! Get rid of a mattress that had supported countless births and a number of agonising deaths all because of a few fleas? And what would we have to lie on?

There wasn't enough money for beer, let alone new mattresses.

Poverty, the Pawn and Drink

The kitchen was the hub of my life; it was the centre of the universe from which all pain and pleasure sprang. In it would be enacted battles both physical and mental. One particular battle happened at least once a week between Kate and myself. It would begin with her saying 'I don't want you to go to school this mornin'.' This should have filled me with joy but it didn't. For it meant only one thing, she wanted me to go to the pawn. I would stand nearly always at the kitchen door leading into the scullery, from which you went by another door into the backyard. I would take up this position as if ready for flight. She would not look at me as she told me why she would have to send me to the pawn but would go about her business of clearing a table, or preparing food, or lifting up the mats, or throwing a great bucket of slack to the back of the fireplace in preparation for the tea leaves that would be put on it to clag it together. And she would be saying, 'It's the rent, I've just got to have it. This is the second week and they could put us in Court.'

Collecting rent cannot have been a very rewarding occupation

Robson Green as the rent collector in the film of The Gambling Man. *'Rory shivered as he walked up the church bank and entered Jarrow... He had six calls in Pilbey Street and fifteen in the Row, and as always when he entered the street he steeled himself, put on a grim expression and squared his shoulders, while at the same time thinking, Old Kean and those other landlords he represents should be lynched for daring to ask rent for these places.'*

in Jarrow in the nineteenth century, and being a cash business it must have carried its own temptations for the collectors. Certainly it did for Rory, the gambling man, as readers of the novel by that name will recall. Here the rent man's patter comes natural to Rory, though very likely his words will have held the same horror for this tenant as being taken to Court for arrears did for our Kate. Kate's debts hung over her head like an avalanche about to plunge down and bury her:

Rory shivered as he walked up the church bank and entered Jarrow. He passed the row of whitewashed cottages, then went on towards the main thoroughfare of Ellison Street. He hated this walk; he hated Saturday mornings; Saturday mornings meant Pilbey Street and Saltbank Row. Pilbey Street was bad enough but the Row was worse.

He had six calls in Pilbey Street and fifteen in the Row, and as always when he entered the street he steeled himself, put on a grim expression and squared his shoulders, while at the same time thinking, Old Kean and those

An Inquiry into Child Welfare in 1909 claimed that 'Many children were very poorly clad and their clothes showed no signs of being repaired and lacked any method of fastening except pins. It was even found at times that a child's under-clothing was sewn on...'

Boots were a mark of status, dignity even. Their absence was not uncommon. Catherine herself did not recall ever having new clothes and was mortified by Kate making her wear a cast-off costume coat of thick serge material, far too big for her, with great ballooning sleeves.

Kate, Catherine's mother, begged barefoot in the streets of Jarrow as a girl and once aroused such pity in a woman that she gave her a pair of boots. Kate had been born in 1882, but in the early years of the 20th century, when Catherine was growing up in East Jarrow, a family neighbour, Mary Ellen Kane, used to come in to borrow Kate's boots. 'Mary Ellen would come to the back door stammering "K...K...Kate. Would you l...l...lend me y...your boots to po...pop into Jarrow?" Kate lent her boots so often that at last she told her to keep them.'

other landlords he represents should be lynched for daring to ask rent for these places.

For four years now he had collected the rents in these two streets. In the ordinary way he should have collected them on Monday, Tuesday or Wednesday because on these days he came this way collecting, and right on into Hebburn, but you couldn't get a penny out of anybody in Pilbey Street or the Row on any other day but a Saturday morning. And you were lucky if you managed to get anything then; it was only fear of the bums that made them tip up.

He lifted the iron knocker and rapped on the paint-cracked knobless door. There was a noise of children either fighting or playing coming from behind it, and after a few minutes it was opened and three pairs of eyes from three filthy faces peered up at him. All had running noses, all had scabs around their mouths and styes on their eyes. The eldest, about five, said in the voice of an adult, 'Aw, the rent man.' Then scrambling away through the room with the others following him, he shouted, 'The rent man, Ma! 'Tis the rent man, Ma!'

'Tell the bugger I'm not in.'

The woman's voice came clearly to Rory and when the child came back and looking up at him, said, 'She's not in,' Rory looked down on the child and as if addressing an adult said, 'Tell her the bugger wants the rent, and somethin' off the back, or else it's the bums Monday.'

The child gazed at him for a moment longer before once more scrambling away through the room, and when his thin high voice came back to him, saying, 'He says, the bugger wants the rent,' Rory closed his eyes, bowed his head and pressed his hand over his mouth, knowing that it would be fatal to let a smile appear on his face with the two pairs of eyes surveying him. If he once cracked a smile in this street he'd never get a penny.

It was almost three minutes later when the woman stood before him. She had a black shawl crossed over her sagging breasts, the ends were tucked into a filthy ragged skirt, and in a whining tone and a smile widening her flat face she exclaimed, 'Aw begod! it's you, Mr Connor. Is it the rent you're after? Well now. Well now. You know it's near Christmas it is, and you know what Christmas is for money. Chews it, it does, chews it. An' look at the bairns. There's not a stitch to their arses an' himself been out of work these last three weeks.'

Without seeming to move a muscle of his face Rory said, 'He's in the rolling mills and never lost a day this six months, I've checked. You're ten weeks in arrears not countin' the day. Give me five shillings and I'll say nothing more 'till next week when I want the same and every week after that until you get your book clear. If not, I go to Palmer's and he'll get the push.'

Kate would not have been put in court for two weeks rent, but often we had outstanding arrears of something between four and five pounds, and as the rent was only about four and six a week they represented many unpaid weeks. So I would be sent to the pawn.

I would go out of the front door with the parcel. It is impossible to imagine the stigma of being seen by the neighbours. Nearly always there'd be somebody in the street doing their step or their windows, and they'd know where I was going. But this was nothing; the real agony started when I reached the bottom of the dock bank where the men waited to be signed on for work. They all knew who I was, old John's grand-bairn, as I was known. Opposite to where the men stood, Dock Street, Bede Street and Hudson Street went off at right angles. Gompertz the pawnshop, known as Bob's, was situated in Bede Street. To get to it I had to pass this gauntlet of men.

How do you assess the agonies of childhood? How do you go about putting them over? As a child I had not acquired the words to fit the pain. But by the time I wrote *The Fifteen Streets* I could give the problem to little Katie:

Katie moved the parcel on to her other hip. It was heavy; but not as heavy as

150

'I had been going to the pawn for some years and was about eleven I think when I asked myself, "Why can't our Kate go herself?" and it came to me that she was as ashamed as I was to be seen going to the pawn. She didn't want to run the gauntlet of eyes either.'

the weight inside her; the weight was leaden. To go to the pawnshop with any parcel filled her with shame; to walk up the dock bank, under the knowledge-able stares of the men idling there against the railings caused her throat to move in and out; and to meet any of her schoolmates on the journey made her want to die; but when it was John's suit she was carrying every tragedy of the jour-ney was intensified a thousandfold.

When her mother asked, 'Will you go down to "Bob's", hinny?' Katie had stared at her, speechless. She wanted to say, 'Our Molly should go, she's bigger,' but she knew from experience that Molly always got less on the clothes than she did, and generally too, she lost something, the ticket, or worse still, a sixpence. And because her mother looked so thin and white when she asked her she remained silent, and watched Mary Ellen go to the box under the bed and take John's suit out.

It seemed such a shame that it was John's, because he had started work

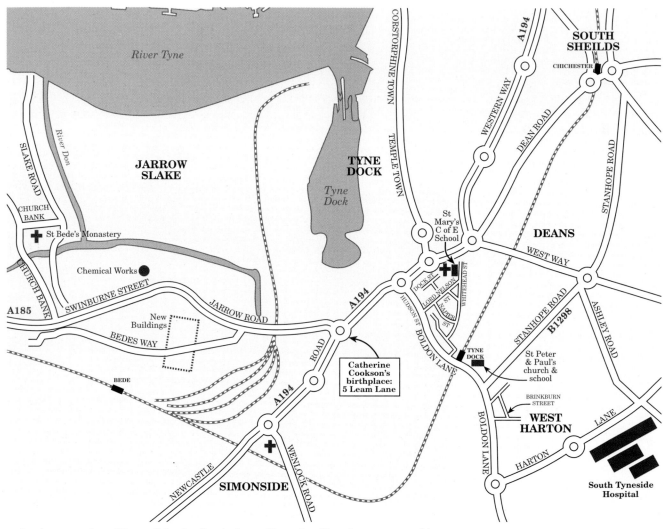

only that morning. They all had, after being off weeks. But there was nothing in the house now to make them a meal, and although they would get subs, her mother was relying on these to pay the three weeks' back rent. Katie felt that once the rent was paid, her mother would look less white.

Going through the arches into Tyne Dock she met Mrs Flaherty.

'Oh, ye're not at school the day?' Peggy greeted her.

'No, I was sick.' Katie stared up into the half-washed face, criss-crossed with wrinkles, and her tone defied disbelief.

'Oh, that's a pity, it is. Ye shouldn't miss you iducation. Some day, when ye're old enough, I'll lend you one o' me books; they'll iducate ye like nothing else will. When ye're old enough that is.'

She snuffled and caught the drop from the end of her nose on the back of her hand.

This is a modern map of the neighbourhood and can usefully be compared with the one on page 42, which shows the area at the time of Catherine's childhood.

Catherine was born in 1906 at 5 Leam Lane, a point where the Newcastle Road meets the Jarrow Road today. This is called Leamlane End on the earlier map on page 42, and indeed the Newcastle Road is still called Leam Lane further south. At the roundabout confluence of the Newcastle and Jarrow roads, there is a plaque commemorating Catherine's birth; another plaque may be found amongst industrial units which stand where the New Buildings once were (just south of the Jarrow Slake). Catherine moved to the New Buildings in 1912.

To the west the Jarrow Road leads to the Barium Chemical Works, pictured on page 119, but this whole area of the Slake is now redeveloped under the auspices of the Port of Tyne Authority and is far better seen from a boat on the river.

The map on page 42 shows the five arches leading east from Tyne Dock to South Shields, the first being a bridge leading to a timber yard, the main four carrying the railway to the dock itself. These were removed in the 1970s, but the area is still signposted The Arches and the road still leads to the intersection with Hudson Street, where the Port of Tyne Authority offices are and where once stood the main dock gates.

The church and school of St Peter and Paul are still in existence, as is the workhouse on Harton Lane, now a hospital.

'Thank you.' For as long as she could remember Katie had been promised one of Mrs Flaherty's books, and the promise meant nothing to her now. She said, 'Ta-ta, Mrs Flaherty,' and walked on, the parcel now pressed against her chest and resting on the top of her stomach.

Although she thought impatiently that Mrs Flaherty was always on about education, she wished her mother was a bit like her. She had almost given up talking to her mother about the examination and what Miss Llewellyn said, for her mother didn't believe Miss Llewellyn meant what she said – last time, she had stopped her talking, saying, 'Oh, hinny, you mustn't take so much notice of things; your teacher's only being nice. The examination she's on about is likely the one you have every year.' And when Katie had sat quietly crying, Mary Ellen said to John, 'Look, lad. I can't go down to the school and see what she keeps on about, I only have me shawl; will you go?'

'What! Me? Not on your life. Now that's a damn silly thing to ask me to do, isn't it! What could I say to the headmistress?'

'Well, will you go and see her teacher, then?'

John had just stared blankly at his mother, then picked up his cap and walked out of the house.

Katie thought the only one who understood was Christine. She liked Christine nearly as much as she liked Miss Llewellyn, but not quite. Life had taken on an added glow since Christine came into it; for Christine made her pinnies and dresses out of her own old ones. She gave her and Molly nice things to eat, too; and she had even given them money, real money, half a crown each. But only twice, for when they took their half-crowns into their mother the second week she made them take them back.

Katie could not understand her mother's attitude of not speaking to Christine and her grandfather. She allowed her and Molly to go next door, but Mr Bracken and Christine had never been into her house since that terrible day some months ago when their mother was taken bad. John and Dominic, too, went next door; and she often sat on John's knee while he and Mr Bracken talked. They talked bout funny things, one of which stuck in her mind: Mr Bracken said you could have anything you wanted if you only used your thoughts properly... There were so many things she wanted, but she wanted above all to be a teacher. Should she do what Mr Bracken told John, lie on her back with her arms outstretched and think of being a teacher until she felt herself floating away? Eeh no! she'd better not, for there were some people who said Mr Bracken was the devil. He wasn't; but anyway, she'd better not do it.

She always had a queer feeling when Dominic was next door, when she would wonder if he were trying to do what he was doing that night she went in unexpectedly. He had Christine pressed in the corner and was trying to kiss her. Her blouse was open, and the ribbon of her camisole was loose. Katie knew that Christine was frightened, for she held on to her until Dominic went out. Then she told her not to mention to John what had happened; and Katie only too readily promised.

At last she reached the dark well of the pawnshop, and listened, her eyes wide and sad, as Bob said, 'Only three-and-six, hinny. It's getting a bit thread-bare.' He turned to a woman and asked, 'Will you put it in for her?' And the woman nodded, taking the penny Katie offered her. Katie wished she were fourteen, then if she had come to the pawn she wouldn't have to pay somebody for putting the stuff in – a whole penny just for signing your name! It was out-rageous, and she disliked the woman intensely for being so mean as to take the penny.

As she was leaving the shop with the money tightly grasped in her hand, Bob said, 'I've got something here that might interest one of your brothers. It'll

Tyne Dock arches, the Hudson Street end: the big building on the right is a dock storehouse, and this side of it, a police box and the dock gates where, as a child, Catherine used to stand. '"Waitin' for your granda?"the policeman would say.'

Hudson Street is off to the left.

154

fit nobody else round these parts. It's a top coat, and it's a bobby-dazzler. Ten shillings, it is. And I only wish I had what it cost when it was new. Tell one of them to have a look in.' Katie said she would.

The Fifteen Streets

In those days the New Buildings held a very mixed assortment. In some cases the contrast was striking, as with the once rich Larkins, who had owned the Barium Chemical Works, further up the road, and who still occupied the two large houses that took up most of the first terrace, and the Kanes who lived at the top of William Black Street – not sixty feet away – and who were so destitute that the daughter not only borrowed our Kate's boots but the mother used to borrow the gully – a bread knife.

Then there were, as in any community, the social climbers. These managed to employ a daily, or send their washing out, or have somebody in to do the washing and the housework. Perhaps I am wrong in calling them social climbers. Perhaps these were just out-ward signs of their respectability.

Then there were the strivers, those who neither drank nor smoked, and whose one aim was to keep their heads above water, water in this case being debt. Then last and by no means least came the hard cases. And there weren't so very many of these cases in the New Buildings in those days. But among them were families domi-nated by drink, as ours was.

From when I was about eight there was scarcely a day of the week that I didn't go down to Hudson Street or even as far as Brinkburn Street in Stanhope Road for the beer. During the War it was scarce and of an evening I would have to stand in queues. By this time I was carrying the grey hen. The grey hen was a large narrow necked stone jar; it was heavy when empty, much heavier full. I carried it on my left hip. True I was given my tram fare back, but I would often walk the whole distance from Tyne Dock to East Jarrow carrying that great jar to save the ha'pennies.

There was a great deal of comment in the New Buildings about my being sent for the beer. It was looked on in some quarters as a disgrace; in the less refined quarters it was termed openly 'A bloody shame, sendin' that bairn for the beer with that great jar.' I think I was the only child in the New Buildings who was sent on such an errand.

As the years went on I became filled with shame at having to carry the grey hen.

Constitutionally my mother was as strong as a horse, yet in some strange way this constitution refused to carry drink, for, from the first glass of spirit she drank, her personality changed for the

worse. After three glasses she became, not our Kate, but someone of whom I was deeply ashamed, whom in my early years I came to fear, then hate, then wish dead, yet all the time loved, loved because she was the only thing that was mine; even while I disowned her in my mind I loved her.

This clash of emotions presented itself to me for the first time one Saturday. I tried to express it in *Fenwick Houses* through Christine Winter and her illegitimate daughter, Constance:

It was a Saturday night and it was summer. I had sat in the back room of the Crown until closing time. There was the usual Saturday night crowd and we had laughed and joked until we parted. Mollie wasn't there, Mollie was never there now. I must tell you about Mollie. But this Saturday night I felt particularly carefree and happy. This wasn't always the effect that drink had upon me now. At one time I could rely on it obliterating all my worries and transforming me, as it were, on to another plane where cares were non-existent and whatever future there was was rosy. Then for no reason for which I could account, every now and again the effect of whisky would be to make me want to argue

Looking south down Hudson Street in 1900, where Catherine went for Kate's beer. Off to the left (unseen) are first Dock Street, then Bede Street (where Bob Gompertz, the pawn, was) and – shown here – Lord Nelson Street. Boldon Lane leads off to the right. You continued up Hudson Street to the Crown cinema – 'up the top, on the right' – to which Catherine 'joyfully escaped' on a Saturday afternoon; beyond lie the railway station (now the Metro) and St Peter and Paul's church and school.

Looking south down Hudson Street in 1999. Lord Nelson Street still leads off to the left, but as the map on page 152 confirms, Bede Street (where Catherine went to the pawn) is no more, and the part of Hudson Street beyond the Boldon Lane intersection (up past the street lamp in the picture) is now a walkway and marked on the map as distinct (see page 152).

and to pick a row with somebody, and this feeling would always be accompanied by a spate of swearing in my mind. I would think in swear words – Mollie's vocabulary wasn't in it compared with the words that presented themselves to me.

The night that Constance brought up my past again was a Saturday night, but I was feeling happy and at peace with the world. I was crossing the bridge in the late twilight, humming to myself the song they had been singing in the back room earlier on: 'Now is the hour when we must say goodbye,' and then I saw Constance. She was standing talking to two girls and I saw her deliberately turn her back towards me. But that did not deter me from crossing over to her and demanding in words that I tried to separate, 'What... what-you-doing-out at this time a-night? Eh? Come on now, away home.' She did not turn and look at me as I mumbled my order, but the other two girls stared at me in a sort of surprised way. I was about to add, 'You, too, you should be at home in bed,' when Constance darted away. I gave an admonitory nod to the girls and walked off, trying to keep my gait steady as I knew their eyes were on me.

There was no evasiveness from Constance once I entered the kitchen; she was standing waiting for me. Her pale skin looked bleached and her brown

Looking north up Hudson Street towards the dock gates in the 1950s. The picture shows the dock gates and adjacent storehouse and (on the left) the offices where the men queued up to be taken on: 'They were the reason why I took the tram from the dock gates to the end of Hudson Street when I was going to the pawn,' recalled Catherine.

Below, a similar view today.

eyes black and staring, and she greeted me with, 'You!... you! You're a disgrace – acting like that on the bridge and Jean and Olive in my class. Oh...h.' The 'Oh' had a weary sound, and she followed it up with, 'I hate you. I hate you. Do you hear?'

Somewhere in my head words were gathering fast but I couldn't get them to come down into my mouth. It was as if there was a gap across which they couldn't jump...

I knew that the greatest disgrace in life was to have a ma who drank. It didn't matter so much if your da drank, most da's did, but to have a ma that drank made people talk about you; like they did about some women in the docks. 'They could drink it through a dirty rag', only the word used wasn't as ordinary as 'dirty'.

Now I must go back to Mollie. She had played quite a part in my life and she

St Peter & St Paul, Tyne Dock. The church was founded in the year of Catherine's birth. She attended the adjacent school from 1916. Here she met stern Father Bradley and kind Father O'Keefe, portrayed in the novels as Fathers O'Malley and Bailey respectively.

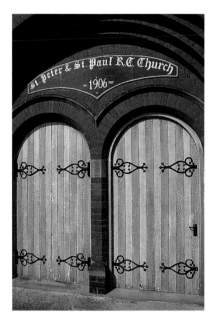

was to play even a bigger part. The simple reason I didn't see Mollie any more was that she had married. Not Jackie, but a very respectable man, a greengrocer, a Mr Arkwright. He was fifteen years older than her and had not been married before, and he didn't like me. It was really laughable when I thought of it, for whatever blame there was attached to Mollie's past he put it down to my influence. There was evidence of my sinning but none of Mollie's. I cannot think that she'd had any hand in forming this opinion, but apparently she could do nothing to alter it, and when she had to choose between becoming Mrs Arkwright and respectability, which position I am sure she never dreamed would be her luck, or keeping our friendship, Mollie, being human, chose Mr Arkwright. She tried to soften the blow by saying he was a bit fussy and wanted her to himself for the time being. She had laughed and nudged me, but I couldn't see the funny side of it. I had met Mr Arkwright three times, and he did not hide his opinion of me. In Mr Arkwright's mind I was one of the fast pieces left over from the war. Moreover, when I had a drink I laughed a lot, which only proved to the greengrocer that he was right in his opinion of me. So Mollie and I no longer met in the back room of the Crown on a Saturday

The Alkali on Swinburne Street, one of the pubs to which Catherine was sent for beer.

night. Nor had I been invited to the wedding. The excuse given me was that it was to be very quiet in the register office. And I wasn't invited to her new home. I liked Mollie; next to my mother, I think I loved her. She had been good to me, she had been my stay in my time of trouble, and her rejection of me hurt more than a little, It absolutely amazed me that she, of all people, could allow herself to be dominated by any man, and it seemed that she was paying a high price for her respectability. But that was the way she wanted it.

Then this particular week, because I had felt so miserable and down, I paid a visit to the Crown on a Friday night, which I had never done before. I had my week's wages on me intact as I had just left the doctor's. It was half-past six when I entered the back room and I noticed immediately that most of the people present were not the Saturday night crowd. There were only one or two that I knew, the remainder being strangers.

I sat down next to a woman called Mrs Wright. She was always a bit of a sponger and soon she was telling me her woes, and I was paying for her drinks. After my third whisky, one of which was a double, I stopped listening and I began to talk. I told her about my job at the doctor's, my clever daughter who could write poetry, which, I assured her, she would one day see in the papers, and I told her about my dear friend who had a farm – Sam's small-holding. At this point we were joined by a man and a woman from a table near by. The man I had seen before. I did not know his name but I knew that he often looked my way. He talked a lot and he laughed as he talked, but his wife had little to say. He stood a round, and then it was my turn. Someone went to the piano and we all sang. And this was the setting when the door opened and

The Alkali, boarded up today, was named originally for its proximity to the Barium Chemical Works on Swinburne Street.

Mollie and her man came in. I was facing the door and I saw her immediately, and with the past lost in the thick vapour of four whiskies I hailed Mollie loudly, shouting, 'Oo! oo! there, Mollie. Oo! oo!' She turned immediately in my direction and after a moment's hesitation she lifted her hand and waved. Then her husband, turning and looking at me for a moment, deliberately took her by the arm and led her to the farthest corner of the room.

Well, who did he think he was? That was deliberate, that was. He wouldn't let her come across, wouldn't even let her speak to me. Who did he think he was, anyway? I threw off my drink.

'What'll you have?' It was the man standing the round again. I looked at him and blinked, and in the act of blinking all my merriness seemed to vanish. I didn't like this man and I didn't like his wife, and I didn't like Mrs Wright. I had spent a lot of money on her tonight and I didn't like her. 'I'll have a whisky – large,' I said to the man.

'You won't, you know, unless you pay for it.' It was the wife speaking, and I turned sharply on her and said, 'I haven't seen you handing out so much.'

'Well! Come on, Dickie. That's the limit that is.' She pulled her husband's arm, and I mimicked, 'That's right – go on, Dickie. Go on before you stand your turn.'

'Now, now.' The man's tone was soothing, and I flung my hand wide and said, 'Oh! get yourself away or she'll hammer you when she gets you in.'

Mrs Wright started to laugh, but I didn't join in. The piano had stopped and people were looking towards our corner, and although the words were whispered I heard a voice saying, 'You shouldn't take it unless you know how

English, 'A job is it? Oh, min skjoun, I could give you a job. Ah yes.' His head went back and he laughed.

'Look, give over, you. Let me go.'

Still peering at her, he said, 'Stop trembling. You frightened? Why do you come here if you're frightened?'

'Please, I... I just want to go. I want to go home.'

'You want to go home?' He was laughing at her again, his face seeming to expand to twice its size. 'All right, min skjoun, we will go home. Ah yes, how pleased I'll be to go home with you.'

'No, no!'

'Aha! Yes. Yes.'

At this moment the door was pulled wide open and another man appeared. He, too, was a sailor and spoke in a foreign tongue, and the bearded man answered in the same tongue, and when the second man emerged into the yard Katie found herself pulled from the wall and pushed forward. And now the bearded man called over his shoulder to the other man, who shouted back apparently in reply. Then they were in the street.

'Which way?' He still had his arm about her, gripping her firmly and forcing her to walk, but when they reached the flare lights outside the pie and pea shop he stopped and peered at her again, saying now, 'Why do you tremble all the time? Why go to the Anchor if you tremble?'

'I ... I went for work; they... I heard they wanted a barmaid.'

'Did I know any Fanny McBrides or Mrs Flannigans? Oh, my... In my early days, in any poor quarter of Jarrow you would see a woman in an old coat and slippers slinking along to the corner shop early in the morning for two ounces of tea, half a pound of sugar and a half a pound of streaky bacon, or something along those lines. Oh, there were dozens of Fannys. And Mrs Flannigans? Oh yes. In any community you'd find upstarts like Mrs Flannigan, and the Mrs Flannigan who lived opposite Fanny in that novel – [Fanny McBride] – wasn't a patch on my Aunt Mary!'

Again his head went back and the street rang with his laughter, of which the passers-by took no notice. A drunken Swede laughing with a woman in the streets at night was nothing new. 'You a barmaid in the Anchor! Ah!' He grabbed her face in his big hand and pressed her jaws in as he said, 'You'd be eaten alive. Do you want to be eaten alive?... No, no.' He answered himself. 'You're frightened of being eaten alive. Why did you want to be barmaid in the Anchor? There are other works you could do.'

'My ... my sister is sick. I've got to look after her; I can't go out durin' the day.'

'No one else to look after your sister? No parents?'

She shook her head.

'You married?'

Again she shook her head.

'You live by yourself?'

'With...with my brother.'

'Why does your brother not work for you then?'

'He's on strike. He's away lookin' for work... '

167

It would seem that Katie Mulholland was fortunate at the hands of her drunken Swedish sea captain, although Catherine herself had reason not to fear the transient dockland population. From the age of seven, when she walked from the New Buildings in East Jarrow to school at St Peter & Paul's, she 'would go through the docks each day and see a multitude of nationalities waiting to be taken on. If they weren't Arabs they were Swedes or Negroes or Russians – those big, burly Russian captains. Not once did anyone handle me, even though at the time there was a tremendous fuss about the white slave trade – girls being picked up and whisked away.'

Before she had closed her mouth on her words she knew she had made a mistake, and he lost not a minute in making use of it. With a nod of his head he said, 'So. So he's away. Well, we go home then?'

'No!' Her voice was harsh now. 'No, no, I tell you. No!'

He did not seem to take any heed of her protest but went on, 'What do you want money so badly for you to go to the Anchor?'

When she didn't answer he brought his face down close to hers and said on a surprised note, 'You sulten...hungry?'

She closed her eyes for a moment but still didn't speak; and when she opened them she did not look into his face but at the top brass button of his uniform, and some section of her mind registered the fact that he was a captain. This seemed to explain the way he talked, for although a foreigner he used his words like the gentry did.

'My God! That's right, isn't it? You're hungry. Come, come.' He now took her by the hand as if she was a child and pulled her through the doorway of the pie and pea shop, and there, in a voice that seemed to shake the ramshackle place, he cried, 'Pies! Half a dozen. Hot. No, one dozen; I could eat half a dozen myself. And peas, two pints.'

'Where's your can?' said the man.

'Can?'

'Aye, sir, yer can't carry peas in a bit paper.'

'That one there, I'll buy it.'

'It'll cost you fowerpence, sir.'

'Fourpence it is. And fill it to the brim.'

The man beside the counter now wrapped up the pork pies in a piece of newspaper, and when he pushed the parcel across the counter the captain, picking it up, thrust it into Katie's arms.

As she held it against her breast she could feel the heat of the pies through the paper and she had a desire to grab one out and thrust it into her mouth. She also had a desire to take to her heels and fly; and she saw her chance as he was paying the man. Once outside the door she could be away up one of the dark alleys and safe, and the pies with her.

She was backing to the door when he turned round, and like someone chastising a child about to do a mischief he turned his chin to the side, while his eyes remained on her and gave that telling exclamation of 'Ah-haa!' Then, thrusting his hand back towards the counter and the man, he received his change and without looking at it thrust it in his pocket. Then his hand groped towards the can; he picked it up and came towards her, and after looking at her hard for a second said, from deep in his throat, 'We go home now, eh?'

He held her with one hand and carried the can of peas with the other, and like this they went through the warren of dimly lit streets and past the black alleyways until they reached the end of Crane Street, and here, pulling him to a halt and her voice full of pleading, she said, 'Please, please don't come any farther.'

'You don't want me to come to your home?'

'No.'

'You're lying. You want me to come.'

'I don't, I don't, I tell you.' She was hissing at him now. 'I just want you to leave me alone. Don't you understand? Just leave me alone. You can have the pies... here.' She thrust them at him. But he ignored her action and said, 'I don't believe you. But, look, we're on the waterfront and near the Middle Gates. There'll be one of your polis men there. Shout. Go on, shout, and they'll come and order me off... Go on.'

She stood breathing deeply and peering at him. She had thought of that herself. She had thought, if I shout the polis'll come. But as afraid as she was of this great bearded man, she was more afraid of the polis. It was when she thought of being afraid of him that she realised she was only afraid of him because of what they would say in the house, her taking a man up there, and what Joe would say if he found out.

She said lamely, 'We... we could walk and eat these as we went.' She patted the bundle of pies.

'But I don't want to walk, I want to go to your home. I want to know where you live... Besides, it would be very uncomfortable eating peas while we walked.' He gave a small laugh now. 'Come,' he said. 'This is your street?'

When she didn't answer he took her arm again, and like someone under escort she walked up the street with her head bowed.

There were people about, but they took no notice of her or her companion.

'Well, it's one thing, you get trained to be quick in big houses, not like this lot here.' She pointed to a tall young woman and a smaller one who were taking down crockery from the hooks on an old black-wood Welsh dresser, the back of which Tilly noticed in some surprise was forming a kind of high headboard to a double iron bed along the edge of which were sitting two young boys and a youth.

'Oh, Ma. Ma!' It was the same laughing protest.

'Are those griddle cakes finished?' Mrs Drew now looked towards a plump child who was kneeling before the fire turning pats of round pastry which were resting on an iron shelf, which in turn was resting on top of a flattened mound of hot ash.

Before the child could answer, Sam Drew, bending over his sister, said, 'She's been scoffin' 'em Ma.'

The small girl, her face red from the heat of the fire, sat back on her hunkers, crying, 'Oh, our Sam! our Sam! I've never touched one,' slapping out at her brother as she said so. And he slapped playfully back at her; then looking at Tilly, he said, 'This lot must look like a menagerie to you.'

She smiled but could find no reply to this. He was right, they did look like a menagerie.

'Well, if you've got a good memory I'll start at the top and work downwards. That one over there,' – Sam pointed to a short, thick man sitting at the edge of the table – 'that's me big brother, our Henry, twenty-four he is, an' married, lock an' chain you know.'

Ignoring his brother's clenched fist, he went on, 'Then there's me next.' He thumbed his chest. 'Then comes our Peg, that one who's slow with the crockery.' He pointed to the taller of the two girls moving between table and the delf rack. 'And then Bill. He's seventeen, him sittin' on the bed, the daft-looking one.'

'I'll daft you, our Sam, if you don't look out.'

'I'm lookin' out, so get on with it.' Sam grinned at his younger brother, then said, 'And his two daft companions, there's Arthur there on the left, he's twelve, and Georgie, he's the one that looks like a donkey about to bray, he's ten.'

'Oh, our Sam!' This came from different parts of the room now.

'Then there's our Katie, who's not right in the top

storey...'

'Oh, you wait, our Sam!'

'And the best of the bunch is Jimmy there. He's a natural scarecrow, aren't you, Jimmy? A penny a day he can earn standin' in the fields.'

'Oh, our Sam! Our Sam!'

'And then there's my Fanny.' He bent and rubbed his fingers in the thick brown hair of the kneeling child, saying, 'She's seven, aren't you, Fanny? An' she's goin' down the pit next year, aren't you, Fanny?'

'Now you shut your mouth, our Sam!' It was his mother turning on him now, no laughter in her face. 'Don't joke about her goin' down the pit. She's not seein' top nor bottom of the pit except over my dead body.'

'I was only funnin', Ma.'

'Well, don't fun about that; the pit's got the rest of yous, but they're not gettin' her. Nor Jimmy there. There's two of you I aim to give daylight to.'

'Aye, Ma; aye, you're right' – Sam's voice was very subdued now – 'tis nowt to joke about.'

Mrs Drew had stopped pouring out mugs of tea and she now looked at Tilly; but for some seconds she did not speak. When she did her voice, although low, held a deep note of bitterness as she said, 'The pit took four of mine in seven years, me man included, so you can see me reason for stickin' out for two of them, can't you?'

'Yes; yes, Mrs Drew.'

'Well now, that said, let's eat.'

It was, Tilly imagined, as if the tall gaunt woman had suddenly turned a knob somewhere inside her being and switched off the bitter memories, for now her voice was jovial again as she cried at her daughter, 'Peg, bring the china cup, we've got company.'

When Peg brought the fragile china cup and saucer to the table and handed it to her mother, Mrs Drew took the saucer between her finger and thumb and gently placed it on the table; then looking at Tilly, she asked, 'You like your tea with milk, lass?'

'Oh yes, please.'

'An' you can have sugar an' all if you like.' This was from the upturned face of Fanny. They all laughed and there was a chorus: 'And you can have sugar if you like' in imitation of the small girl, and she, swinging her head from side to side, exclaimed, 'Aw yous! you're alway scoffin', yous!'

'And now we're all here we'll start. I said, we're all here' – Mrs Drew now looked again at Tilly as she placed the china cup and saucer before her – 'except there's my Alec. He's on a double shift – it's the water down there – he'll be dead beat when he does come up. Shouldn't be allowed, twenty-four hours under at one time! and he only a bit of a lad.'

'He's eighteen, he's older than me an' I've done a double shift.'

'Oh listen!' Sam held up his hand. 'Hero Bill's done a double shift.' He leant towards his younger brother now, saying 'Aye, but it wasn't in water standin' up to your neck.' Then, his tone altering, he said, 'Somethin's got to be done. By God! somethin's got to be done.'

'Now! now!' It was his mother's voice again. ''Tis Sunday, we've got

'Oh, for the eternity of childhood time
When the morning was New Year's Day
And dinner-time was high summer
And evening was autumn
Falling into December and bed...'

company, no more pit talk.'

Since only nine could be seated at the table, two of the younger boys, Arthur and Georgie, remained seated on the bed, and when their mother ordered them to come to the table to get their shives, thick slices of bread with a piece of cheese in the middle, she looked from one side to the other as they approached and said, 'You don't deserve nowt either of you; 'tis a wonder you're not in jail.'

'Why, what have they been up to?' Henry, the married son, said, turning his head towards them. 'What's this? What have you been up to, you two now?'

When they didn't answer he looked at his mother and she, evidently trying to suppress a smile, made her voice sound harsher than ever as she said, 'What have they been up to? Just tried to burn the Myton's place down, that's all.'

'What!'

There were splutters from different members at the table. Some of them choked, so much so that Katie had to be thumped on the back before their mother went on, 'They were scrumpin' apples an' one of the gardeners caught them, an' being kind to them instead of taking them up to the house an' then callin' the polis, he thumped them well and roundly, bumped their heads together, kicked their backsides and set them flyin'. And what do you think they did last night as ever was?'

'Well, what did they do, I'm waitin'?' Henry asked.

Again the table was convulsed with laughter, and it was Sam who now said, 'They stuffed straw up half a dozen drainpipes, you know the old trick, an' set fire to them.'

'No!'

'Aye.'

'At the Myton place? Oh my God! I wish I'd been there. Eeh! you young buggers!' He turned and looked towards the bed where the two boys were sitting with their heads hanging but with their shoulders shaking with laughter.

'And not content with that' – the mother nodded at her eldest son – 'they went back into the orchard and helped themselves to apples, not windfalls this time but from the trees. My God! when they told me that I was

sick. To try a second time! God! they're lucky they weren't caught. Anyway' – she grinned now – 'three good stones of them they brought in. As they said, they could have brought a cartload 'cos everybody was too busy pullin' the burning straw out of the drainpipes.'

'They'll end up in Australia those two.' It was Sam now nodding towards them.

'They'll never live to reach Australia.'

As Tilly watched Mrs Drew's head move slowly back and forward there was rising in her a swirl of merriment such as she had never felt in her life before, and when Mrs Drew ended, 'Swing they will, the both of them, from the crossroads an' we'll all have a field day,' the laughter burst from her throat. It surprised not only herself but all those at the table, because they had never heard anyone laugh like it. It was a high wavering sound that swelled and swelled until, holding her waist, she turned from the table and rocked herself. She laughed until she cried; she couldn't stop laughing, not even when Katie, herself doubled up with laughter, put her arm about her and begged, 'Give over. Give over.' Nor when Sam lifted her chin and, his own mouth wide, cried, 'That's good. That's good.' And he kept repeating this until he realised her face was crumpling and that the water running down it was no longer caused by merriment; and so, straightening up, he looked round the table and raised his hand, saying, 'Enough is enough.'

The noise in the room gradually subsided, and Tilly turned to the table again and, her head bowed, murmured, 'I'm sorry.'

'Sorry, lass? You've nowt to be sorry for. We've never had such release in this room for many a long day. It's good to laugh, it's the salve for sores. Aye, it's the salve for sores. Drink your tea, lass.'

Gratefully now Tilly drank her tea. Then she looked at the sea of faces about her, warm, caring faces, and she thought she had never felt such closeness as there was in this family. Most of them spent their lives underground, even the girls; but there was a happiness here that she envied, a happiness here that she longed to share. She looked across the now silent table at Mrs Drew as she said, 'It's lovely tea, lovely.'

Tilly Trotter

'We played ma's and da's
Those years ago:
Ma's apron and skirt,
Da's shirt and old bowler;
Round the top corner
In the chimney breast
We played at houses,
In which the test
Was birth.'

Nearly every night after tea, and when I had been for the beer, I went out to play for a while. Winter or summer we would play round the street lamps, or outside Cissie Affleck's shop.

There were certain parts of the New Buildings we selected for play at certain times of the year, as also we did our games. In the winter, towards Christmas, it was usual to gather around the shop, for then, Cissie would be putting the Christmas decorations in her window, and if you were in the Christmas Club you could stand for hours pointing out what you were going to get. A shop with real scales, and bottles, and a counter; a doll...a black doll perhaps, or boxes of chocolates, or a long gauze stocking filled with an assortment

177

of useless things. And in between gazing and planning we would skip or play tiggy, or Jack, Jack, shine your light.

In *Kate Hannigan* Rosie Mullen was Annie Hannigan's best friend. Rosie was two years older than Annie, but much shorter. She was a replica of her mother, being dumpy and fat, with small bright eyes and a round face. Her dark hair stuck out in two-inch plaited points from behind her ears. She looked ugly and quaint and likeable, and Annie had a deep affection for her... It was half past eight on Christmas Eve morning when Annie, sitting in the back-yard lavatory of the Hannigan's house, heard a scramble of feet in the Mullen's yard next door. Their back-door banged and her own opened, and a plaintive voice chanted up the yard 'An-nie! Are-ya-comin' out? An-nie! Are-ya-comin' out?' Together, the two girls set off to take Nancy Mullen out in the pram.

Rosie grinned broadly, and taking hold of Annie's hand, dashed with her into their backyard, seized the big, dilapidated pram, in which a two-year-old child lay sucking a dummy, and pushed it out into the cobbled back lane, down

'Girls were playing the summer game of bays, hopping on one leg, their bare foot pushing the clean-cut bottom of a glass bottle from one chalk-marked paving square to the next; boys in groups according to their ages, were playing chucks in the gutters; and here and there a bare-bottomed young child crawled on the hot pavements.' The Tide of Life

'*"Ooh! Ain't they luverly?" said Rosie, gazing in rapture at the display.*' Kate Hannigan

'*In the winter, towards Christmas, it was usual to gather around the shop, for then, Cissie would be putting the Christmas decorations in her window, and if you were in the Christmas Club you could stand for hours pointing out what you were going to get.*'

Children playing ball behind Croft Terrace. '*Kate worked up Croft Terrace; the way they are dressed shows that this is not a poor area.*'

which they hurried, the pram tossing about like a cork on the ocean, past seven back doors with their accompanying coal and oozing lavatory hatches, round the bottom corner, across a piece of waste land where children were already playing among mounds of dirty snow and wet, brown grass, and into the front street of the houses opposite their own. About half way up, one of the houses suddenly changed its pattern; above its window a large, yellow tin placard said, DRINK BROOKBOND'S TEA, and a gay old gentleman on another piece of tin asked you to look at him to see how fit he kept on ALLY SLOPER'S SAUCE. The house window itself held tier on tier of bottles of sweets receding away from the gaze of the beholder to dim regions beyond, while, balancing on

A glimpse of South Shields market where Thrift Street and King Street meet. Many would wait until last thing Saturday to get cheap meat that was going bad.

'... She next went to the bacon stall, and her searching eyes coming to rest on some scraps, Katie pointed to them and asked for a pound.

"That lot throopence hapenny, lass," the man said.

"Thank you." She nodded and put her hand into the bag for her purse. Then, her two hands tearing the bag open, she let out a yell that made the stall-holder jump and those nearby turn and gape at her. "The purse! the purse! It's gone. Oh, my God, it's gone."'
Katie Mulholland

the front of every shelf, were boxes of hearts-and crosses, sherbet dips, ever-lasting stripes, scented cachous and jujubes. In front of the window were large jars of pickled cabbage and pickled onions, and seven-pound jars of loose jam and lemon curd. Among these, at crazy angles, were placed Christmas wares of 'Shops with real scales', dolls in the minutest of gauze chemises, work-boxes, miniature boxing-gloves and tram-conductor sets of hat and ticket puncher. Paper-chains hung in loops from the ceiling, together with huge red and green paper bells, of a honeycomb pattern. From the chains and bells, held by fine threads, dangled swans, balls, dolls, ships and fairies, all in fine glass and painted a variety of colours.

Annie and Rosie pushed the pram against the wall and joined the other two children, who were endeavouring to get a first-hand view by hanging on to

The old Co-op warehouse on the Tyne awaits demolition. The Co-op movement can be traced back to the 18th century and by 1830 there were 300 co-op societies in Great Britain, including (but not only) consumer stores.

In the late 19th century, however, there was still little variety in the shops and far fewer proprietary brands than today. Basic stuffs, like butter and sugar, would be made up in a shop, sold in weighed amounts from casks or kegs. Soap was soap and not, at that time, presented in all manner of perfumes or packets. In the early 1880s, however, two massively expensive advertising campaigns – for Hornimans tea and Holloways pills – began to change all this. Their impact was revolutionary.

the high window-sill by their elbows and sticking their toes into the wall...'Ooh! ain't they luverly?' said Rosie, gazing in rapture at the display.

Kate Hannigan

Courting and Cavorting

In the summer, we would usually gather on the open space before the terrace, or on the slack bank and the timbers. The big timbers were tied together with sleepers to which ropes were attached allowing each timber some leeway. When the tide was high and the timbers were floating you ran over each one, pressing it down into the water and jumping on to the next before your feet got wet. This was called playing the piano. Or we'd make tents and play houses, or gather round Richardson's top corner and into the chimneypiece and play shops, or bays on the pavement, what others called hopscotch. And then there was diabolo, and scooters, and rounders, and hot rice, and ...knocky-door-neighbour. Some nights we would get dressed up and go singing in procession round the five streets.

We were only following our elders in this, for like a spring fever, there would come at certain times of the year among certain women of the buildings, among whom were Kate and Mary, a madness, a jolly madness, that would force them to dress up in any old clothes, and singing and beating tin cans, parade around the five streets. I've seen Mary leave her washing and Kate her baking and, getting into the men's clothes, go dancing round the doors, and she solid and

Ships at port; a group of fisher girls lighten the day with sailors on a British warship on the Tyne, around the time of the First World War.

sober. There was a primitive weirdness about this which I recall whenever I hear the Kerry Piper's song.

Sundays were a sort of respite to me, but boring to everybody else in the house, because, not having best clothes, they couldn't go out. I connected Sundays with big dinners, everybody going to bed in the afternoon – and Cissie Affleck, because nearly always I watched Cissie and her young man taking their weekly walk after Church on Sunday afternoon.

You could almost tell the time from Cissie and Mr Maitcham passing along the slack bank opposite the end of our street on a Sunday afternoon after chapel Sunday school. I can see them now. He was a tall, well-dressed, superior looking man. You couldn't put the prefix lad or boy to Mr Maitcham. I think he must have been about thirty at that time and Cissie in her early twenties. There they would walk, keeping a specified distance apart; sedately, even regally they would pass by the New Buildings. I cannot ever remember Cissie casting her eyes across the road to where, at the corner of Philipson Street, was her shop. No, this was Sunday. A day for Church and courting, a prim kind of courting. You didn't wear your heart on your sleeve in those days. Couples didn't fling their arms about each other in public, even go as far as kissing in public, that was left to the darkness of a back lane, or better still some place up the country, and courting in the front room was only sanctioned by the, morally speaking, broad parents, and this, as was well known, led to a quick

'In Shields there were the most beautiful girls. I don't know what it was, whether it was the sea air or what, but their complexions were beautiful.'

wedding and evoked the remark 'Well, what d'ya expect. It was askin' for it.'

But I could never connect the front room or a quiet spot up the country with Cissie and Mr Maitcham, and as for the back lane, never.

A little later, I managed to give time to falling for a lad. There were, I remember, Willie Birket and Tot Lawson, but I made headway with neither. Tot had dreamy eyes but they didn't look at me and in an endeavour to turn them in my direction I gave bullets to his sister Ruby to pass on to him. They had no effect on his eyes. But when I was nineteen he sought me out and he became my lad, for a while.

In my school days I cannot remember any lad ever giving me a bullet, I was the one who preferred taffie or bruised fruit.

On one classic occasion I spent my little hoard on a deceiving male. His name was Eddie Youlden. He sat behind me in Standard Four, and I thought he had made a song up about me

'I love a lassie,
A bonny, bonny lassie;
She's as pure as the lily in the
dell...'
Pure as the Lily

that he kept singing down my neck. It went:

K-K-K-Katie,
Beautiful K-Katie,
You're the only g-g-girl that I adore.
When the m-moon shines on the cow shed,
I'll be waiting at the k-k-k-kitchen door.

I'd passed him bags of bullets before I realised I was being deceived. Never trust a ginger headed man.

Conditions of Life

All of the health statistics for Tyneside compared unfavourably with national averages and with the record of other industrial areas. When the national infant mortality rate was 32 per 1,000, the Jarrow figure was more than 62 per 1,000. Why was the local record so bad?

Certainly overcrowding played a big part. Overcrowding had been defined in 1981 as more than two adults to a room. Children

Despite Health Acts in the 1870s food retailing was still very much a matter of caveat emptor. *In* Tilly Trotter Widowed, *Noreen Brentwood, pregnant by Tilly's son, works in Proggles of Newcastle: 'The lamps fixed to the walls on each side of the table were so placed that they illuminated only the table itself and the double oven fireplace exactly four feet from the end of it. Perhaps this was as well for they shut out from Noreen's gaze a regiment of cockroaches and fearless rats that infested the margin of the basement... The two cats that should have been parading the premises were so satiated with food that they slept.'*

under ten counted as half and babies under a year old not at all. Under this definition a two-roomed dwelling could contain any combination of adults and children between four adults and no children, and one adult and six children (plus any number of babies), without beng considered overcrowded. Still in 1921, 14,782 (42.3% of the population) lived in overcrowded conditions in Jarrow.

Our house was hardly ever without lodgers. Sometimes they would sleep on the feather bed in the bedroom with me Uncle Jack. Then me granda would sleep in the brass bed in the front room, me grannie on her couch opposite him, and Kate and I would be turned round, me granda and me grandma sometimes having the feather bed in the bedroom, and four lodgers sharing the two beds in the front room. For one short period I remember Kate and I slept at Mary's, while the saddle in the kitchen was taken up by Uncle Jack. At another period there were five men sleeping in the front room, one on a shake down.

In the nineteenth century, sanitation was as inadequate in rural areas as it was in the townships. *The Girl* is set in the fictitious village of Elmholm, but this description of its state in the 1850s attests to reality:

Elmholm village, setting for The Girl: *'It consisted of forty-five houses. These included the two short rows of miners' cottages, which were situated behind the houses on the right hand side of the village green... Their middens had been in front of their doors, to the disdain of the artisans of the village who kept their middens at the back of their houses.'*

Two-room Northumberland, cottage, 1910. Picturesque as it looks, in the nineteenth century of Hannah Boyle (The Girl) *and Tilly Trotter such cottages were far from ideal. In the little mining villages through Northumberland and Durham, poor sanitation and ill-health was as much a problem as in the Tyneside towns.*

'Beyond the stretch of moor-land lay a huddle of houses known as Rosier's Village. They were mean, two-roomed, mud-floored miners' cottages housing the workers in the mine that lay half a mile beyond... Even when he was well past the village the stench of it still clung to his nostrils.'
Simon Brentwood in Tilly Trotter

It consisted of forty-five houses. These included the two short rows of miners' cottages, which were situated behind the houses on the right hand side of the village green if you were journeying from Allendale towards Sinderhope. They had been built some fifty years previously to house the overflow of miners then employed in the lead mines and smelting mills. They were low two-roomed stone dwellings with mud floors, except where flagstones had been laid down; and at first the sanitary habits of their occupants had been similar to those which prevailed in the town of Allendale itself; their middens [dry lavatories] had been in front of their doors, to the disdain of the artisans of the village who kept their middens at the back of their houses, or better still at the bottom of their gardens. But time had wrought change so that now not only were all middens to be found behind the cottages but for most of the year the villagers all lived peaceably together, except on days such as fair days, or the Friday after the pays. This was the day on which the miners received their accumulated pay. Then the rowdiest among them fought, cracked each other's heads, and beat up their women. The return to normal wouldn't take place until work started again.

The Girl

In *The Glass Virgin*, the middens are 'a series of big holes in the ground and a number of mounds'. But in East Jarrow at the turn of

'*In our house the lavatory was a dry one,*' recalled Catherine, '*[but] you could be aroused by the back lane hatch [see right] being lifted and the scavenger rudely thrusting in his long shovel.*'

Kate Hannigan: '*The only time Annie got a violent distaste for it was when the men unexpectedly lifted the back hatch to clean it out with their long shovels. Then a revulsion for it would overcome her. She didn't like the scavengers, nor would she follow the cart with her companions, shouting:*

Cloggy Betty, on the netty On a Sunday morning...'

the century, real progress had been made! In our house the lavatory was a dry one – a misleading term – with a long wooden seat with a hole in the middle and, if you kept the lid on, it was a wonderful place for musing and meditation. Once having made yourself comfortable you looked out through a space between the top of the door and the framework on to the grey, sloping, slated roof that covered the wash-house and the staircase of the upstairs house, and if you were lucky you saw a grey bird hopping about – we called them grey birds because we didn't know their real names. Here you were shut in and became lost in a world apart, a secret world. That is, if the lid was on. If it wasn't and you fell into a state of musing, which often happened, you could be aroused by the back lane hatch being lifted and the scavenger rudely thrusting in his long shovel. Many a time has this catapulted me from the seat to hide my face against the door, leaving my bottom exposed.

From time immemorial the streets of Newcastle and Jarrow would have been loaded with horse muck, attracting flies that spread disease, and although Public Health legislation in the 1870s extended the scope of sanitary authorities, house sanitation remained primitive well into the twentieth century. One tends to forget that improvements in sewerage or the water supply – and utility operations of any kind – cost money. Today we are accustomed to central government as Lady Bountiful, but then any progress came from the rates, from the local people.

In the following piece, Katie Mulholland describes the awful conditions in what was regarded as a well-kept, working-class home in the 1860s:

'Ma! Ma! What's come over me. You know what I forgot?... Me pay.' She swiftly undid the two buttons of her dress, unloosed the tape that tied her bodice, then thrust her hand inside the neck of her chemise and unpinned the calico bag. Her breath was coming quickly and she gabbled now, 'You wouldn't believe it. That's all I've thought of for days, getting me wages, and I couldn't get home quick enough, but since I come in the door I haven't thought a thing about it. Would you believe it?'

She bent her slender body towards Catherine and pressed the calico bag into her hands, and Catherine slowly took the four shillings out, looked at them, then swiftly she opened her arms and drew her daughter to her, and as swiftly she pushed her away again. Unclenching her fist and holding out her palm with the money in it, she said in a voice that was cracking slightly, 'You must have a shilling back every month.'

'A shilling, Ma! No, no, I don't want a shilling.' Katie's voice was high and she shook her head from side to side. 'The threepence will do. Mrs Davis has got a half a crown saved up for me, now; I don't want a shilling.' She

Tributary of the River Allen, lead mining country, setting for The Girl. *Typically – one of the major health hazards was nature's water supply.*

'"Ty...typhoid? God! how... how did we get that?..."

Dr Arnison turned and pointed to the bucket standing on the table.

"The watter?"

"Aye, the water... Where do you get it from?"

"She draws it mostly." He now jerked his head towards Hannah, then demanded, "Where did you get it from?"

Hannah looked at the doctor as she said quietly, "I always put the bucket under the ripple that comes out of the bank, never into the stream."' The Girl

pushed her mother's hand away, and so quickly that the money spilled on to the floor, and immediately she was on her hands and knees picking it up. One of the shillings had rolled into a mud-filled crevice between two of the stones, and when she dug her finger in to get the coin she disturbed the earth and a strong

A woman, more than a century ago, carries two buckets of water, steadied by a wooden frame, from the river to her home in Allendale.

obnoxious smell rose to her and filled her nostrils. The smell in the house was always worse in the summer when the water from the middens seeped under the foundations and oozed upwards.

When the four coins were retrieved they all laughed. Katie now opening the back door, stood under the lean-to and rinsed her fingers in the wooden tub of water that stood on a bench attached to the wall.

Katie Mulholland

One of the major health hazards was the water supply. In the nineteenth century the sources of supply lay in the river, in wells, and perhaps most safe of all in rainwater gathered domestically in barrels. In *The Dwelling Place* Matthew actually invents a system which pumps water out of a burn to be carried to sluice out the water closets. But it doesn't save him:

In 1846, when William married an apothecary's daughter from Shields, Matthew built him a fine house, standing in a half acre of land within a quarter of a mile of the mill itself. It had a large kitchen and parlor, three bedrooms and a garret, and besides the washhouse, coal-house, and stable there was, of course, the new sanitary arrangement – even better this one, for the effluent didn't flow back into the river as it was too far away to pipe it, but into a huge cesspool; nor was their fresh water supply drawn from the river but from a well that Matthew had caused to be sunk at the bottom of the garden.

It was around this time that Matthew became really conscious of the

Eighteenth-century dwellings of the Allendale lead mining community in Northumberland. Disease was a constant possibility.

danger of the river water, for it was into this that the effluent flowed, that cattle paddled and went to drink, that cats and dogs were thrown, and it was from this also that most of the hamlets and the villages drew their water supplies.

The fact that the river was fast running in parts failed now to convince him of its purity, for all along its length it was being used as a dump for filth.

It was in 1844, when typhoid was seeping both sides of the river from South Shields to Gateshead and from North Shields to Newcastle, that Matthew's mother and grannie were taken, and also Nellie. Nellie had been thirteen and bonny and bursting with health, but she had been snuffed out like a tallow-candle in the wind, whereas Annie, who had always been weakly and who, too, had lain with the fever, survived. There was no accounting, they said, for the workings of God. All man could do was to bow before His will. Matthew had let his pass, and concentrated on the river.

But in 1849 when his only daughter, the one child that Cissie had given him, died of the cholera at the age of eleven, he did not let it pass, but cursed God. He cursed Him in private and in public; he cursed Him to the face of his great friend, Parson Hedley... And he cursed Him to the damnation of his own soul, so said the righteous when, two years later almost to the day, after rising up from the laden Christmas table, he died.

He had left the table and staggered to the settle because of a violent pain in his chest, which he said wasn't like wind for he had hardly commenced to eat. An hour later, still sitting on the settle, strangely enough where the miller before him had drawn his last breath, he died, and more strangely still, of the same complaint...

The Dwelling Place

There are many reasons given for Tyneside's poor housing and health record compared to other emerging industrial townships of the nineteenth century. Perhaps, in the end, it was simply a question of priorities: expansion, not health or hygiene, was the main priority of these 'frontier' towns. It was the lure of rich new coalfields, for example, that provided the impetus for a healthy water supply:

For years men had failed to discover whether coal lay beneath the apparently impenetrable magnesian limestone layer of the East Durham plateau. The solution, after much costly failure, came with the development of powerful steam pumps. This equipment then proved equal to the task of bringing clean water from deep underground for drinking.

Only with this breakthrough in the 1850s did the drawn-out development of a decent domestic water supply begin in earnest: first to a tap that served five or six homes, then to a tap for every backyard, and finally, in the twentieth century, to people's homes.

4 STRIFE

In 1877, those who were enlightened by reading newspapers discussed among other things such topics as Disraeli proclaiming Queen Victoria Empress of India and seeing to it that she had the adulation of Indian princes and African chiefs. But for the ordinary man and woman in towns such as South Shields, there were other happenings that struck nearer home, very much nearer home.

The sea which provided most of the inhabitants with a livelihood also created havoc and disaster. There was that awful night in December last year when three

'The sea provided most of the inhabitants with a livelihood.'
Left: part of the Shields fishing fleet today.
Right: the North Shields fish market and leading lights – the huge white towers that fishermen once lined up to ensure safe passage into harbour.

vessels were wrecked and the sea, still unsatisfied, had engulfed and destroyed another two later in the day, and all under the eyes of horrified townspeople who could only watch helplessly. Even though the Volunteer Life Brigade did heroic work, many lives were lost.

Such tragedies had the power to unite the townspeople, at least for a time. Rich and poor alike mingled in their sorrow until the poor, once again forgetting their place in God's scheme of things, protested against their lot. And how did they protest? They protested through societies called trade unions.

Since the first national union of the Amalgamated Society of Engineers had been founded in 1851, in every town in the country where skilled workers were employed trade unions had sprung up, to the fear and consternation of the middle classes who looked upon them as a network of secret societies, whose sole purpose was to intimidate honest citizens, plot to confiscate their property, cause explosions and mob violence and bring the country to total revolution if they were allowed to get the upper hand.

The County of Durham was a hotbed of such people. They agitated in mines, steel works, in shipbuilding yards, in factories, and it was even whispered they tried to inveigle young women into their ranks; and not only those, let it be understood, from the common herd, but women of education and property.

The Gambling Man

One such woman of education and property was Theresa Rosier, who had been reared in the very cradle of capitalism by the powerful influential mine owner, George Rosier, a man capable of declaring that he'd see his striking workforce 'gnaw their arms off...before they get the better of me'. She appears to us first in the opening page of *Katie Mulholland*.

Theresa took after her father, at least outwardly; whom she took after inwardly they had yet to discover, for whoever heard of a mineowner's daughter going to a chartist meeting.

[The Chartists championed the social and economic grievances of the working class through petitioning for political reform. Feargus O'Connor was an extremist leader of the organisation.]

The Rosiers had thought they had heard the last of Chartists in 1855 when that madman O'Connor had died, but there was an element trying to revive itself in Newcastle and their own daughter had attended a meeting and dared to voice her views at the dining table. That any girl of seventeen should talk back to her father was unheard of, but that she should bring into the open a matter that was like a gaping wound in his side was so monstrous that she had feared on that

particular occasion that Mr Rosier would collapse. And if this wasn't enough, her own brother had espied her, three miles away on the fells, talking to groups of evicted miners from the village, trouble-makers, men who were more like savages and brutes than human beings. At the sight of his sister degrading her-self Bernard's rage had been almost as great as his father's. To use his own words he had thrown her into the carriage. Mr Rosier had confined his daughter to her room for a fortnight, and she, her mother, had had to bear the brunt of his tongue. What, he had demanded, had she bred him, a viper? A viper indeed.

Theresa doubted whether she would have come to her present way of thinking at her age without the tutoring and guidance of her governess.

Ainsley had been a forcing house, like the one over there near the green-houses where Mr Wisden, the head gardener, performed miracles on plants with a stove-pipe. Ainsley had been her stove-pipe, and she thanked God for her... Ainsley had taught her to see things as they really were.

She had been five years old when Ainsley came into her life. She could remember the day when she first saw the tall, thin woman and realised that Ainsley was plain-looking. That was before she became aware that she herself

'The man pointed his thin dirty finger at John. "We'll have to hang together, that's the solution. The bloody unions will have to find out whose side they're on. Why aren't they up in London doing some-thin'? There'll be riots afore long, you'll see."'

It wasn't just the men who rose up against their masters, as is shown in this picture of striking fish curers, nor was it only women from the workforce who protested. Prototypes for those twentieth-century champions of female suffrage led by Emily Pankhurst found vehicles for expression in both the Chartist and Union movements.

was saddled with the same complaint. Ainsley was thirty when she came to Greenwall Manor. She was forty-two when she left it, on the day following their secret, exciting visit to the meeting on the Newcastle Town Moor, when the cavalry came and rode into the thousands of people, and they had run with the rest, and almost been trampled to death. It was there they had been seen by Mr Careless, a magistrate and friend of her father's.

Ainsley had been turned out in disgrace and without a reference. For who could give a reference to a governess who had corrupted a young mind? That's what her mother had said. Her father had said much more and his language had been much stronger, for had not the woman made him a laughing-stock by inveigling his daughter to attend Chartist meetings, and making her an open sympathiser with the rebel and scum in his own pit?

Ainsley had refuted nothing her employer had accused her of, and she had dared to stand up to him and say that she was proud she had enabled one of his family to think for herself, and that he, too, should be proud that he had one intelligent person among the dunderheads in his household.

She had known what it was to die when she saw Ainsley being driven away from the door. She hadn't been allowed any word with her; she was locked in her room, but she had hammered on the window and Ainsley had lifted her joined hands towards her. They said, 'Be strong.' She had tried to be strong, but it was difficult without Ainsley's support. She had begun by proposing setting up a weekly class in the village to teach the miners to read and write. When her mother had recovered sufficiently she had said, 'Child, do you think a miner would go down a mine if he could read and write correctly? Do you

*'To hear our Katie talking about
the unions you would think their
members had been bred in
monasteries, all the men are so
good, honest, upright individuals,
all fighting their wicked masters.
Mind, I'm not saying that some of
the masters don't deserve that title
and they need to be fought...'*
The Mallen Girl

want us to starve? Never let such a proposal come to your father's ears, it could
cause him to have a seizure.'
Katie Mulholland

These women were, not least in their courage, prototypes for those
twentieth-century champions of female suffrage led by Emily
Pankhurst.

People ask me what I think of the feminist movement today,
and I have to disappoint some of them by saying that I do not agree
with the way the movement tries to denigrate men, to take their
manliness away.

Certainly my women characters are strong, they always come
through, but that is because they are me. I have had to be strong all
my life, from the time I was a child I have had to contend with fear:
I feared God, hell and damnation, and the priest's admonitions from
behind the grid of the confessional; I feared Kate's drinking to an
exaggerated extent and feared going the same way as her; and then,
for ten years, I had to contend with the breakdown. Now, I am capable
of doing everything that I make my characters do: good, bad or indif-
ferent. I am quite capable of doing the worst things possible.

But I would never condone a matriarchal society. I have always
worked with men and I have always preferred to do so, though the
men I work with are associates, not bosses. I will not have bosses!

Them vrs Us
It might be expected that in the later part of the nineteenth century,

STRIFE

What did I want from life?
Gaiety, riches, happiness,
Not strife.
Why not strife?
Again I say why not strife?
For at this stage of your age
The only wisdom you have gleaned
Has been sucked from strife:
Fighting through trammel,
Through fear, sickness, pain,
All generated by strife,
Has taught you that life,
To be a vital thing,
Must be bred on strife,
It is the yeast to knowing, growing,
An understanding of the decades
Allotted to your share,
Of the being in you you cannot
*   touch, but hear*
And fear to know more in case you
*   see yourself bare.*
Strife has been your friend;
Do not desire to finish your last
*   days alone.*

the working class was all set to rise up as one against its industrial masters. But in fact the only example of working class solidarity came during ten days in the middle of May, 1926 – the occasion of the General Strike.

Of course many strikes did take place and some were marked with considerable violence, but through inter-union conflict and squabbles over demarcation lines (between boilermakers and ship-wrights after the revolution wrought by the John Bowes, for example), the unions consistently failed to present a unified front, or even to convince the majority of workers that they should join them. In the great engineering strike of 1871, for example, only about ten per cent of the striking workers actually belonged to unions.

This conversation between Katie Mulholland's brother Joe and the older man, Mr Hetherington, shows the mixed feelings among the workers and hints at the inter-union chaos.

They remained silent for some minutes until Joe, trying to turn the conversation, said, 'What do you think about the movement, Mr Hetherington?'

'What do I think about it?' Mr Hetherington took a bite out of a meat sandwich. 'I think it's comin' to a head, lad.'

'You think there'll be a strike?'

'It's as near as damn it, but none of us wants it.'

'Have they put the petition to the old man?'

'Aye, but things are different now.' Mr Hetherington put his head back and looked up at the tangle of gear attached to the grimy roof. 'They've changed; the whole place has changed since it went over into a company. I've seen the day when you could go to the old man an' talk to him. Aye, even me. Many's the time he's stopped by me side an' said, "What do you think, John? Is it an improvement?" He was always out for improvement, makin' things better and better.'

'Well, he still is, isn't he?'

'Aye, yes, but at a price. He hasn't got the hundred per cent backin' of the men he used to have in the old days. You can't get at him, or any of them up top for that matter; they're working from London now instead of the works here, although the bloody place is so full of offices and staff now we'll soon have to move the blast furnaces.'

Joe laughed at this but continued to look at Mr Hetherington – he liked to listen to the older man talking – and Mr Hetherington went on, 'See what they've done to the puddlers. Given them a ten per cent cut, and the whole country has accepted it like sheep – that is, all but North Staffordshire. They're standin' firm and they've come out.'

'Do you think the puddlers'll support them, Mr Hetherington?'

'No, lad, I don't. There's too many unions, too many heads of unions, too many bosses, too many under-bosses. It's every man jack for himself, or his

own little band, instead of them all joining up together. After all, we're all steel men. But God knows we don't want any strikes; I've seen enough of them in me time.' On this Mr Hetherington rose to his feet, saying, 'Well now, here we go, lad. Let's see those rivets flyin'.'

And all day Joe helped the rivets to fly until the buzzer went at half-past five. He had entered the boiler shop in the dark and he left it in the dark. But that didn't trouble him; he had seen the daylight through the grimed windows of the shop, and at dinner-time he had sat on the river bank where the skeleton ribs of a ship were rising from the keel, and with his mates he had talked ships, talked 'Palmer's' with as much pride in the firm as if he was one of the share-holders getting his ten per cent.

Palmer's men might fight, and argue, and talk against the bosses, even against the old man himself, but they were Palmer's men, and underneath it all, proud of the title.

Katie Mulholland

It wasn't always easy for the union bosses in the mining industry either. For when new coalfields were opened up (for example in East Durham in the 1820s and '30s and on the Durham coast in the 1900s), groups of workers, each accustomed to widely varying working

Left: Some of the 93 Boldon Colliery Putters arriving at South Shields County Court to answer breach of contract summonses. Moves to educate working men posed a threat to some leading industrialists: 'Theresa had begun by proposing setting up a weekly class in the village to teach the miners to read and write. When her mother had recovered sufficiently she had said, "Child, do you think a miner would go down a mine if he could read and write correctly? Do you want your father's business to collapse? Do you want us to starve?"'
Katie Mulholland

conventions and conditions, would converge on these important new sites from many different places. The workers' different conventions and conditions were absolute tinder for internal industrial disputes, and posed a fundamental distraction from the overall solidarity of purpose.

Outsiders like to brand all workers in the North East with similar personalities, needs and aims, as members of one group of like-minded people called the working class. Out of that comes the myth that the real conflict was a class conflict: strife between 'them' and 'us'. In fact the struggle was as much 'us vrs. us' as it was 'them vrs. us'. Take a look at *The Fifteen Streets*; the magnifying glass of the novelist cannot lie. If it did, who would believe what my characters do and say?

There were those who did not live in the fifteen streets who considered the people living there to be of one stratum, the lowest stratum; but the people inside this stratum knew that there were three different levels, the upper, the middle, and the lower. All lived in 'houses' either upstairs or down; but in the lower end each house had only two small rooms, and upstairs or down the conditions were the same – the plaster on the walls was alive with bugs. These might only appear at night, to drop on the huddled sleepers, but that strange odour, which was peculiarly their own, wafted through the houses all the time, stamping them as buggy. No one went to live in the lower end unless he was forced. To the middle and upper fifteen streets the bottom end was only one step removed from the workhouse, for its inhabitants were usually those whose furniture had been distrained or who had been ejected from their former houses for non-payment of rent.

There were three nightmares in the lives of the occupants of the middle and upper fifteen streets. And these were linked together: they were the bums, the lower end, and the workhouse.

In the middle houses there were four rooms...boxes, generally, but boxes that were divided, giving privacy of a sort to one or two extra beings. The upper end had only three rooms to each house, and these were either up or down. Here, water was not carried from the central tap in the back lane but from a tap at the bottom of each yard. This stamped the area as selective, automatically making it the best end.

Upstarts

Not only did these more subtle social divisions exist, but if anyone tried to cross the demarcation line he would very likely be vilified for being an upstart.

Like Angus in *The Round Tower*, I was an upstart and was called an upstart. Here, Angus is about to rise in the world but will find it more difficult than buying a few smart shirts:

As the back gate opened there came the sound of a train whistle and it seemed to pipe Emily Cotton into the house. She came in backwards, thrusting her thick, firm buttocks against the door and from her arms she dropped on to the table an assortment of garments, exclaiming 'There! What do you think of that lot?'

'Oh, Mam! Look at the bread.' Rosie retrieved the loaf from underneath the clothes, then swiftly began picking up one article after another. Holding a jumper up in front of her, she said, 'Oh, this is all right. What did you give for it?'

'Threepence.'

'Here, I got you a couple of shirts; they'll do for work for you.' Emily threw two garments towards her son and he caught them, and without looking at them he threw them on to a chair, saying, 'I've told you, Mam, I don't like wearin' other blokes' gear.'

'You were bloody glad to wear other blokes' gear, let me tell you, once on a time.'

'Well, I'm not any more, Mam; so don't get them for me.'

'God!' Emily Cotton lowered herself into a straight-backed chair and lifting one foot slowly up on to her knee she stroked her swollen ankle vigorously, and it was to it she addressed her remarks as she said, 'Talk about out of the frying-pan into the fire, I've spent most of my bloody life with upstarts. That lot along there; their noses in the bloody air so much they have to have their necks massaged. And now I come to me own house and me son tells me that he's got too damned big to wear another bloke's shirts. Let me tell you,' she lifted her head to him, 'you'll never be able to buy shirts of that quality in your lifetime. Let me tell you that.'

Angus stared at his mother for a moment. Then, the corner of his mouth moving upwards, he went towards her and, leaning forward, put his big hands on her shoulders and brought his face down within an inch of hers and said, 'Emily Cotton, that's where you're wrong. One of these days I'm goin' out and I'm goin' to buy six of the best bloodiest silk shirts in all this bloody town, and I'm going to wear them for work just to let them see.'

Religious Divisions

And there were other divisions, which were always much more powerful than class and which gave scope for the most terrible cruelty and bigotry.

Me granda was a Catholic who never stepped inside a church door, but would strike a blow for the Pope, yet at the same time scorning and decrying the Richardsons and the McArthurs, close neighbours, who were strong practising Catholics. Pulling them to shreds almost daily, he would hold them up as a sample of everything that was bad. He despised them as he despised all churchgoers, yet it was he who insisted that I was to go to a Catholic school.

The temperance movement was strong in those days. Shops would open selling cocoa in an attempt to reform people's drinking habits.

A variety of temperance societies were established by the end of the nineteenth century, often allied to churches and chapels. This culture offered a demonstrably advantageous alternative to the one which expressed itself in drink, prostitution, irreligion and poverty, and it gave its participants a leg-up in society irrespective of class.

'Chapel people had power, they could get people done out of their jobs, she had heard of it happening.'
The Tide of Life

I was the only one who ever dared to argue with him, but one day I had to run for it. I was about thirteen at the time and I was quite concerned because of the fate of my Protestant friends, for I had a lot of nice Protestant friends and the fact that they were all going to end up in hell worried me. It had been hammered into me that there was no hope for the Protestants, simply because they were Protestants. If they were sensible and changed their coats then they could be assured of eternity in heaven; if not, it was the devil and hell for them. From an early age I developed the faculty of seeing two sides to everything and one night, after listening to a particularly bitter haranguing against the Protestants, my imagination running wild, I saw most of the neighbours in a state of undress being forced to sit on hot grid-irons – because that is what happened to you in hell – and my mind protested and said it wasn't right. The following day was Sunday and on my return from the first session of praying for me granda's soul I passed the Salvation Army standing outside the line of bars opposite the Dock gates, openly proclaiming their allegiance to God. I saw them as a courageous group of people and I knew that I wouldn't have the pluck to stand in the open and acknowledge my God. This filled my mind all the way home and when I got indoors I answered the unintentional brain-washing of years by saying, without any preliminary lead-up, 'I like the Salvation Army, they've got pluck.'

I can see his face now. It seemed to stretch at all angles until it covered the whole fireplace and was as red as the blazing coals that were cooking the gigantic Sunday roast.

'What did you say?' His voice seemed to come up through the floor boards. I ignored the wild signalling of Kate from the scullery. She, I knew, thought I had gone clean doo-lally-tap, but nothing could stop me.

'The Halleluyahs aren't afraid to praise God in the open.' I went on, 'And another thing, they don't go to Church and then come out and get drunk.' Of course the last bit didn't apply to him because he got drunk without going to church.

'GET OUT!'

'You'll not frighten me like you have everybody else, so you needn't think...'

Kate saved me by dragging me by the scruff of the neck into the scullery, and from there pushing me into the backyard, the while hissing at me 'Have you gone stark starin' mad? What's come over you? Stay out for a minute.'

As I stood at the bottom of the backyard I heard him yelling, 'Salvation Army, now, is it? Did you hear her? Begod! we'll have her comin' down the street next knocking bloody hell out of the big drum, or sitting at the harmonium at the street corner leading the lot. You'll see.'

And you know, I think he was a bit afraid of what I might do if driven too far, so for a while, at any rate, there was no tirade against the Protestants.

In such a community as this, innocent people got hurt. In *The Blind Miller* it was Sarah whose only sin was to love a chapelite, David Hetherington. But as Ma Ratcliffe takes great comfort in pointing out: 'Stink-pots like the Hetheringtons couldn't be expected to walk this way with wedding rings.':

All along Sarah had known it would come to nothing – what hope was there for a Catholic and a chapelite? It was a greater barrier than a social one. The Hetheringtons might live in the fifteen streets, but the gap between her family and them was as wide as being a prop man in the docks and one of the managers living in his big house down Westoe end in Shields.

From the film of Colour Blind. *Bridget, a Roman Catholic, is pregnant by James, a Protestant Negro, whom Bridget has married in a Register Office, thereby transgressing virtually every tenet of so-called respectable society!*

Just as often the hurt would rebound on the bigot. In *Fanny McBride*, as we have already seen, the redoubtable Fanny eventually rejects her favourite son, Jack, for marrying a Protestant, and spends the rest of her life regretting it.

All the neighbourhood had been laughing up their sleeves at what was going on, and not one of them daring to tell her. And they were wise, for she would have laid out anyone who dared to come and say that her lad, Jack, was courting a Hallelujah on the sly; for whoever heard of a Catholic taking up with a Salvation Army piece?

Divisions of Race

The Arabs were introduced to Shields in the crews of sailing ships in the nineteenth century. By the First World War as many as half the crew of a ship might be Arab. As a child I took their presence for granted and didn't register the difference between Arabs and us especially because, from the age of seven when I started at St Peter's and St Paul's School, I would go through the docks each day and see

An Arab-owned, seaman's boarding house in South Shields' Corstorphine Town.

a multitude of nationalities waiting to be taken on. If they weren't Arabs they were Swedes or Negroes or Russians – those big, burly Russian captains.

Not once did anyone handle me, even though at the time there was a tremendous fuss about the white slave trade – girls being picked up and whisked away.

But among our people were those who relished the luxury of condescension in a community where there were few luxuries of any kind. Race, like class and religion, was an opportunity not to be missed.

In this extract from *Colour Blind*, Bridget, a Roman Catholic, is pregnant by James, a Protestant Negro, whom Bridget has married in a Register Office, thereby transgressing virtually every tenet of so-called respectable society!

An Arab procession through the streets. In Colour Blind *the priest tries to correct Rosie's view of Arabs: 'Look at me, Rosie, for I have something to tell you... Has no one ever told you that God is colour-blind?'*

A bairn coming. Kathie held her head between her hands. A black bairn. For it would be a black bairn, she was sure; there was too much of him in comparison with Bridget's whiteness. The child would be black both inside and out, and her Bridget would have to push a black bairn around the streets. Mother of God! How could a daughter of hers stand up under the shame of it? She rocked her head with her hands. But Bridget didn't seem to be ashamed: there she was, away now in Shields, walking openly with him in the broad daylight! Hadn't she watched her go down the street with never a look to right or left, her head

The Mill Dam Riots in 1931.

'"There's always been trouble down there," she went on. "Look at that Saturday a few years back, when the Arabs rioted around the shipping office and stabbed them three policemen."

"You couldn't only blame the Arabs for that," Cavan put in sharply; "it were our blokes agitating them not to sign the P.C.5 form that did that, together with those bloody Arab boarding-house masters who bleed them dry... It was the white agitators and the black masters who caused the shipping trouble, I'm telling you..."' Colour Blind

held high as if she had something to be proud of? What had come over her? Why had she done it? Kathie beat the top of her head with her fist. Would the good God tell her why she had done it?

Something of the same question was passing through Bridget's mind as she faced the look of ill-concealed scorn in the eyes of the shop assistants. She had watched her husband put down the five pounds deposit and sign his name with a proud flourish on the form which was an open sesame to a choice of oil-cloths, of beds and bedroom suites, of half-sets of china and Nottingham lace curtains. Never had she dreamed that she would be mad with the joy of it; but there was no spark of joy in her, only pain and pity, and gratitude and abhorrence – the pain and pity and gratitude were the feelings that the bulk of towering blackness evoked in her; the abhorrence was for herself and the thing she had done.

When they left the shop it was her husband who showed her out. Taking the door from the hand of the shopwalker he stood aside to allow her to pass. But the closing of the door did not shut out the tittering from the shop, and its sound brought an angry flush to Bridget's cheeks, and a higher tilt to her chin. They laughed at her because he treated her like a queen! If she had married one of them she would have been made aware of her inferiority for the remainder of her life, and if she had married one of her own class never would she have known the meaning of worship – not to speak of consideration; never would she have known what it was to be loved as this man loved her. Then why was she ashamed of him? Why did it take all the rallying of her forces to brave the streets with him at her side?

When they were together, closed in by four walls, with no eyes upon them, the shame would fade, and then a strange tenderness for him would fill her. Even at times a feeling she thought might be love for him would sweep over her. This often happened in the night when he woke her with his loving, for even with his passion, which lifted her into realms hitherto unknown, his love-making never lost the adoring quality that gave to it a gentleness. But she wished again and again that he would not show this gentleness to her in public, for it was this as much as anything that brought the guffaws and smiles of ridicule upon them. She wanted to tell him, but she could not bear to hurt him. She had soon found that she could hurt him with a look or a word; and she knew that she must never do this... she must never hurt him more than she had done by marrying him. She did not blame him for marrying her – if she had been in her right senses it would never have come about – Matt had always warned her... Matt... She shuddered. She had Matt to face yet. Oh God, give her strength for the day when Matt would speak to her, and drag from her the reason why she had done this thing...

As they turned into Dunstable Street James spoke a cheery 'good morning' to a small group of men standing at the corner. They answered him in low growls, turning their heads away and becoming engrossed in each other's conversation.

And Bridget felt a desire to stop and shout at them, 'He's as good as you – he's better than you. He wouldn't let his wife trail round the bars after him to get what was left of his pay; nor yet have his beer if the bairns went naked – you lot! What are you, anyway?... Scum...scum.'

She was shivering when they entered the empty house; and James, all concern for her, said, 'I know you got chill, honey – come, we go to your home – there's a big fire there... You love me, Rose?'

She nodded.

'Always?'

She nodded again.

'No other man, ever?'

She shook her head.

'Not when I'm away at sea, like some white women?'

'No, no, never that!' Her protest was vehement.

His enormous lips traced the outline of her face. The moving black blur filled her with such conflicting emotions that she became faint under them. His unfinished words ran into one another, forming a lulling drawl. 'Rose love... my beautiful Rose. No other woman in world like you... You marry me 'cause you love me. You don't mind colour, and our baby... my baby, she be a girl; we

The Mill Dam Riots in 1931.

*'The only wisdom you have gleaned
Has been sucked from strife.'*

call her Angela, eh? like angel... Rose Angela.' His fingers moved down the waist-band of her skirt and pressed gently on her stomach. 'I feel her heart-beat... she'll be like you, Rose... white and beautiful with long limbs and...'

The sound that checked his words was of someone breathing. They both remained still, pressed close against each other for a second longer, listening to the hiss of the in-drawn breath. James turned slowly, but Bridget almost jumped into the centre of the kitchen at the sight of the priest standing in the front-room doorway.

If it had been an ordinary man, James would have demanded 'What the hell you up to eh?' before, perhaps whirling him through the air into the street. but a priest to him was not a man, so he said with laughing irony. 'Why, sir, you near scared me white.'

The priest looked from James to Bridget, and the expression in his eyes bore down her courage. Her head dropped and the old childhood fear of him overcame her.

'I told you to bring him along to the vestry.' Father O'Malley might have been speaking to an animal, and his words seemed to have been pressed thin in their effort to escape his tight lips.

'I... I didn't tell him, Father.'

Colour Blind

Aloneness

Later Bridget imagines 'that once inside the fifteen streets she would find a measure of peace and protection among her own kind; but when she thought this, the enormity of her crime in all entirety had not been brought fully home to her...it needed the return to her own class to do this.' God help you if you earned exclusion from the community and dared to remain in it. Illegitimacy was not unheard of in the Tyneside of my youth but it provided a tempting challenge for the bigoted poor. One day one of the girls in Philipson Street was having a birthday party. I hadn't been invited but I knew I would be. I knew I was going to that party because hadn't all my playmates been invited? There they were now, all going towards this particular backyard door. But the funny thing about it was that they all passed me without even looking to the side I was on. I might have been a brick in the wall for all the notice they took of me. They had their best dresses on; some had pinnies over the dresses. They all wore nice hair ribbons, and each carried a little parcel.

When the last one had gone I still hadn't moved, but when I thought I heard Kate's voice calling me I went swiftly down the back lane, keeping close to the wall, past the low lavatory hatches, past the higher coal hatches, until I came opposite this back door. And there I stood looking towards the upstairs window. And as I stared there came into my body a riot of feelings, anxiety, disappointment, urgency, all churning round a sort of breathless desire. I stood with my mouth open, panting. I had to get into that party, it was imperative that I got into that party, because I had never been to a party except once when I was five when I went to a birthday party in Mrs Lodge's in Leam Lane. But I only remember the occasion because my Aunt Mary had put some pearl beads on me, her own beads and I had snapped them, and I got a spanking for my pains. We had parties, I have described them, but this party was different. It had been talked about for days, even weeks. There were going to be lovely cakes on the table, all kinds of lovely cakes, and then games and carry-on. I had to get into that party.

I knew what had happened. Mrs X had forgotten to ask me... I knew it wasn't girls who picked who were coming to their parties, it was their ma's who said, 'You can have that one, and that one, and that one.' I knew I had only to attract Mrs X's attention and I would be in at that party.

I could see the outline of figures moving backwards and forwards behind the lace curtains so I set about attracting the attention of one of them. I jumped up and down, I did lot of Ooh, ooh, oohing! because I knew that if any one saw me they would tell Mrs X and she would come to the window and say, 'Aw, there's little Katie McMullen. Why,

'It was in the spring of 1929 I left the North, sad yet hopeful; sad because I told myself I was never going back. I had finished with the North and all it stood for.'

come on up, Katie. Fancy me forgetting about you. Come up, hinny.'

But my antics attracted no one to the window. The back lane was empty. There was no one in the whole wide world for me to speak to. There descended on me a feeling of desolation, of aloneness, it wasn't to be borne. I ran across the back lane, pushed open the yard door, went up the stone steps to the staircase and knocked.

At this point memory dims. I seem to see one figure after another coming to the top of the stairhead and looking down. Then the hostess herself came towards me. I can see her face now, round, flat-looking, full of self-importance. But she deigned to bend towards me as she whispered, 'You can't come up. Me ma says you can't.'

Perhaps I was foolish enough to ask 'Why?' I don't know but I do remember her next words.

'Well me ma says you haven't got no da.'

Children need no preliminary lead-ups to vital statements, they simply make them. I turned from her, closed the door quietly, went down the stone steps, out of the backyard, across the back lane and up our backyard.

I am not sure whether I am the first person to use this word 'aloneness' to mean something quite different to 'loneliness', but I tried to capture what I mean in *Fanny McBride* when, at the end, the whole family stays away except for Philip, the son whom Fanny never really liked because he was an upstart. The image I recreated there I owe to a great friend of mine called Mannie Anderson, a Jewish doctor from South Shields. After I left the North and began to write I would be invited back occasionally to give talks, and would stay in Shields with Dr Anderson. What impressed me about him was his sheer dedication to the patients in the Infirmary: in the middle of the night, if necessary, he would go to them and comfort them. And one day he told me that what saddened him most of all were those patients who had big families but for whom no visitors would ever come. At visiting time in the ward they would just sit there staring into space, knowing no one cared. His description stayed with me and touched a strong spring in myself. I understood what those patients felt and I knew I had to bring it out in my work:

When Philip stood looking down on her, she pulled herself to her feet saying nothing, then angrily pushed the chair to one side and shambled to the light which she switched off before saying shortly, 'Get yourself to sleep!'

Without a word now he went into his room, and in the firelight she groped her way to the bed and, sitting on its edge, she began to rock herself back and forward, back and forward. And after a while her rocking ceased and she was about to slide to her knees on the floor and implore God of His mercy to take this lonely longing from her heart when her whole body was consumed by a furious anger. It rushed through her like a torrent sweeping a gorge. The anger cried out against God, against her entire family, against this son [Jack] that she loved more than anything on earth. What had she done to deserve such treatment? Hadn't she given him everything? With every ounce of her flesh and every fibre in her heart she had given to him, depriving the others of love to give to him, and what thanks had she ever got from him? But she had never wanted his thanks, only for him to laugh with her, joke with her, tease her, as if she was a bairn or lass, and for that small return she had given him every-thing, her life, the whole of her life. Damn and blast him! he was an ungrateful swine...an unforgiving swine. Blast him to hell!... She hoped...she hoped... There was a great lump in her chest like a weight of iron. It rose, pressing itself upwards into her throat. She gripped her neck to suffocate the sound that was endeavouring to escape, then as the tears spilled from her eyes she turned and pressed her face into the pillow. So intense was her emotion that it seemed to her that she was crying through every pore of her body, for the whole of her huge bulk was aching with a queer ache like a cramp, and as a cramp will converge to one spot all the aching gathered itself into a knot in her side where the wind usually was, and so intense did the pain become that it even stilled her crying, and she slowly straightened herself up, her hand gripping at the flesh under her breast. She tried to call out to Philip, but there was no sound in her throat.

She knew she was in her chair by the fire again, but she couldn't remember moving from the bed. The pain had stopped. It had been shoved away by a blackness that for a brief moment terrified her and checked her breathing. She was now lying in the blackness. It was as if a mighty hand had been placed over her mouth and eyes and even over her inward sight for she could see nothing, not even in her mind.

Slowly the fear of the darkness left her and she lay in it, almost calmly, waiting as she had been doing all night, and for days and weeks past, waiting, waiting. And when at last the darkness slowly lifted and she was able to glance once more about the firelit room, she noticed a very odd thing, so odd that, to put it still in her own words, her heart nearly shot out of her mouth, for sitting in the other armchair right opposite to her, literally dead to the world, was herself.

With a strange lightness upon her now she rose from her chair and moved nearer to the great slumped figure and stood staring at it in a kind of awe for a moment. Begod! she wasn't a pleasant sight, not a bit like she thought she was. She stroked down her apron, as if in an attempt to put a semblance of tidiness on herself, and the thought struck her that it was...queer...it was, that she could do this, make herself tidy...yet that other one of her was not affected by it. As she raised her eyes and looked slowly around the familiar room, with every detail clear and distinct before her eyes, although there was nothing but the dim light of the fire to show them up, it came to her with a sort of great pity, over-whelming pity, that she had died, died in that spasm of pain and anger and

'I will succeed I simply cannot fail; the only obstacle is doubt...

'At the age of twenty-three I got the post of laundry manageress in the workhouse at Hastings...if my fate was to work in a laundry then I would one day manage the biggest in the country.'

doubt, and all her waiting was over, all the recriminations, all the worries of being left alone. Everything she had tired herself out with these past months had been a useless waste of good time.

The 'Escape'

This feeling of aloneness grew into a concrete thing. Hard and painful, this feeling of rejection was to gather to itself, as time went on, shame anxiety, remorse and bitterness. But even as a teenager it exercised a positive power in me, a power which, at twenty-three years of age, was to enable me to escape the North East altogether.

When I was thirteen I had an accident in the school yard which left me immobile for some time. I remember the day when I stood on my two feet alone once more. I can see myself limping out of the bedroom and leaning for support on the white scrubbed kitchen table and looking through the window down the length of the yard. The yard door was open and I could see into the back lane, and there passing was Florrie Harding and Janie Robson and as I watched them I said to myself, 'I'll never play with them again.' I did not know childhood had left me, but remember saying to myself, 'What are you going to do?' and that this question was accompanied by an odd feeling in my chest. It was a mixture of many feelings, the feeling that I had when I went to the pawn, and when I carried the grey hen; the feeling I had when I humped the coke sack on my back; the feeling I had when I passed some of the other girls on the road with their nice clothes on while I was wearing an old costume coat of Kate's that reached to my knees and bulged out like a balloon from my hips – the feeling I had of being different.

But this day I resolved to do something about it. I said, 'Well, I can only do two things, I can write and I can do housework.' There was no lack of ideas or even complete stories, the impediment was the mere matter of grammar and spelling. This, as I have explained in my introduction, I rectified as soon as possible. And so it was some ten years later that I left the North and all it stood for. Hopeful because I was going to make something of myself. In my case I carried notes from Lord Chesterfield and a page torn from a cheap magazine. I still have that page.

I will succeed I simply cannot fail,
The only obstacle is doubt.
There's not a hill I cannot scale
Once fear is put to rout.
Don't think defeat,
Don't talk defeat,
The word will rob you of your strength.

'I will succeed', this phrase repeat
Throughout the journey's length.

The moment that 'I can't' is said,
You slam a door right in your face.
Why not exclaim 'I will' instead,
Half won then is the race.
You close the door to your success
By entertaining one small fear.
Think happiness, talk happiness,
Watch joy then coming near.

But the truth is that you cannot escape your roots. There is a need to come back. It's in most people, but it's much stronger in the North East than many areas.

The politicians in the South find it difficult to understand why the people of the North will not leave their homeland if they cannot get jobs. If a child in the South does well at school he'll make light of the decision to move away in search of a job. Certainly this was the case in Hastings: if a boy had big ideas he'd move to London, no problem about it. But people up here, they might hate each other within the family, they might hate each other from one town to the next, but if anything happens it's the North East against the rest.

'The day I went up to the New Buildings, East Jarrow, and saw William Black Street was no more.'

To Tishy, who was in her first year as a teacher at the secondary modern, the solution was to move away, get out of the North East. 'The trouble with us in this corner of the globe,' she said, 'is that we are too insular. Metaphorically speaking, everybody in the North East has the chummy back lane, back-to-back mentality. People won't move. If they do it has to be within easy reach of the town in which they were born. If they go farther afield they develop symptomatic phobias.'

The Invisible Cord

The day I went up to the New Buildings, East Jarrow, and saw William Black Street was no more, a deep sadness overwhelmed me. I stood on the rubble where the kitchen had been, that kitchen in which all the emotions of life had been enacted, and memories flooded back to me. But in that moment the most vivid one, strangely enough, was my granny.

I've talked a lot over the years about our Kate and me granda, but not much about me granny perhaps because she died when I was seven years old, but on this particular occasion memories of her came flooding up so poignantly that the tears rolled down my face and I went back to the car and wrote down the vivid impression I had got of her.

Me granny sat in a wooden chair
She had a stiff face, wrinkles and straight black hair,
But if I ever needed comfort I found it there.
Between her knees each day she'd have me stand,
And look me head for nits, and I'd play the band
Until she said, 'Here's a bullet
Mind you don't choke yourself
It'll stick in your gullet.'

I went home sad, my mind filled with nostalgia for the days that had been, for the days that I once ran away from, from the North as it once had been – when I was little Katie.

Eventually, upstart that I was, I had to face the fact that I wouldn't write a word that anyone would really want to read until I threw off the pseudo-lady and accepted my early environment, me granda, the pawn, the beer carrying, the cinder picking, Kate's drinking, and of course my birth, for it was these things that had gone to make me. Also, to own to being a Northerner and all this implied. It was this cathartic outlook that set the pattern for *Kate Hannigan*, my first novel. I once wrote a piece called *Time and the Child*, which seems to sum it up:

I can smell my memories of childhood. The smell of real manure from a farm-yard, as opposed to that from chemicals, recalls the scene of a farm outside Shields. I was on high ground. There were rocks and the sea to the left of me, and there away in the distance was a field of corn.

On closer investigation I found that the edge of the field was rimmed with fragile flowerheads, hundreds and hundreds of them. Kate later told me they were poppies. I thought the name didn't suit them somehow, they should have been called flamers; and there was no incongruity in the fact that this is what me granda called the people next door.

Perhaps it's old age creeping on or galloping on but I find my mind going back to these days to episodes in my childhood, more and more.

Here I am seventy-one and I know that inside I am still very much the child, the child that was Katie McMullen of East Jarrow, only the façade is the woman and it hasn't the power to control the child. Somehow I can't ignore the power of the child I once was and still am. I am still hurt as she was hurt. I still laugh as she laughed. I still have the secret insight that she had, the insight that recognised sorrow and loneliness in others, the insight – that was in me before I sucked milk, for, as our Kate said, if I in her womb had been aware of what she was suffering during those nine months that she carried me, then I should surely have been born mental.

Well, I must have been aware of her pain for I nearly went mental, didn't I?

I find that time is galloping away now; it isn't dawn before it's dusk. The hours leap into days and days disappear into weeks, and I can't remember what I did in them. The pity of it is, my mind at this stage is clearer than at any period of my life, and I long for time, long time, the time of childhood, in which to expand and grow again.

You know, we are what our early environment makes us. I believe that is true. All through our life those early years colour our thinking. No matter how thick the veneer, heredity has a way of kicking itself through the skin. When the race is almost run and the two ends of the circle are meeting you see the child coming towards you, and you go back into his time more and more. You can recognise his thinking more so than when at twelve, thirteen or fourteen you left him behind. The knowledge of his magic is fresh before your eyes, for in his time of being there was no growing, there was no age. You knew people did what they called dying and although they were put into the earth they had gone into the sky; but you were here, there'd be new bread for tea, it was Saturday the morrow and there was no school. Sunday, you'd have to go to Mass. On Monday...When was Monday? There was no such thing as Monday, not on a Friday night. Monday wouldn't appear until late on Sunday night when you were dropping off to sleep. And Sunday was a long, long way off. It came after Saturday. But tonight was Friday and tomorrow you would go the penny matinee at The Crown. What greater joy could anyone ask for?

In that time I can smell baking day in the kitchen. I can see the kitchen as if it were set out before me. There's me sitting on the fender, Kate bustling all around me.

'Move your backside out of that,' she says.

I shuffle along the steel fender away from the black-leaded oven door, quickly past the fierce blazing fire built up in a slant you know to keep the heat against the oven, and when I reach the far end of the long fender I say, 'A...w!' for the steel is always cold between the end of me knickers and the top of me stockings.

I watch her lift the sneck of the oven door and pull out the oven shelf on which there are four loaf tins; she plonks the shelf into the fender, dextrously upturns the loaf tins that are as black as the oven itself, gives three taps with her knuckles on the bottom of each tin, nods towards the oven as if acknowledging her debt to it, then looks at me and says, 'Have your got your yule-doo ready? Come on, look slippy if you want to put it in. I haven't got all day.'

I can see myself coming out of my dreaming, jumping to the table, picking up the much fingered piece of dough I've shaped into a man – perhaps this time he has currants for his eyes, mouth and nose, and a row for his coat, or perhaps this time funds were too low for currants and his face was featureless and his suit without buttons. I can see me laying him tenderly on the hot plate. I want to straighten him out, but Kate's voice will have none of it.

'Don't make a meal of it, not yet anyway. Out of me road!'

The oven door bangs on my yule-doo, Kate straightens her back, dusts the palms of her hands loudly against each other, blows a strand of hair from

'The truth is that you cannot escape your roots. There is a need to come back...

'When the race is almost run and the two ends of the circle are meeting you see the child coming towards you, and you go back into his time more and more.'

her sweating brow by thrusting out her lower jaw and puffing upwards, then she looks down on me and says gently, I can hear her saying it gently, 'Well, that's done, we'll have a sup tea, eh hinny?'

'Oh aye, Kate. Aye, yes.'

The smell of new bread slides me back into eternity, the eternity that was childhood; the eternity of pain and fear and that sick feeling in my chest caused by fear; the fear that me granda would make a big hole in his pay by dropping into the North Eastern pub before coming home.

The fear that he might have had a very good week and so they'd all have a drop too much, and there'd be divils fagarties later on.

The fear there'd be no money on Monday for the rent; and I'd be kept off school to go to Bobs – Bobs was the pawnshop.

The fear that I'd have to miss Mass on Sunday 'cos me boots weren't decent.

The fear of facing the headmistress on the Monday and admit I hadn't been to Mass. Oh, that fear outdid the one on purgatory, hell and damnation.

But, as I said, there were moments of wonder when all these fears were forgotten – in that everlasting time by memories of flamers in a field, and smell of new bread in that kitchen that served so many purposes, and the memory of which will stay with me till I die.

I wrote in my introduction, 'Isn't it strange that from the wider world into which I escaped I have to return, like the eel to the Sargasso Sea, to die where I began, among my ain folk.' As a young woman I would go to eleven o'clock mass on Sundays at St Peter's and St Paul's, but in this my eighty-first year I no longer have superstitions about life and death. I see death as a long sleep, and if it isn't a long sleep it'll be a nice surprise.

IIn the last few years the blood disease which has been with me all my life has brought me to the depths and I have been ready to let go. On January 18th 1975 I wrote the following: I felt very ill yesterday. The feeling continued into the night: I couldn't sleep. My Siamese twin self-pity, was in charge. This was a real bout of mental exhaustion. For months now it has been a fourteen hour day, seven days a week, up at half-past six in the morning trying to get through my ever growing mail; the day allotted to the phone, visits from agents, editors, photographers, interviewers and, just recently, the BBC Unit. I tell myself it can't go on, but it does.

Lying there in the dark last night with Tom by my side I asked myself what I wanted, and strangely the answer was – joy.

Some months ago I felt so bad, bleeding so badly, that I made the decision to give up writing altogether. Believe me I have to be bad to do that. I was in a desperate state, feeling that I was about to let go. And I went to this place, and I said to whatever was there that

Ferry Landing, South Shields.

I was tired and just wanted to give up and let go.

But as I said it I thought, why do I ask? Because I know from experience that I will never get the answer that I want. Never do I get the sympathetic answers: 'Yes, you're right. This is what you should do. It's about time you thought about yourself.'

Instead it was as if someone had come to my side, and then went for me – 'You're going against your nature. All right, if you give up, you'll give up and you'll go. You'll go very quickly because it isn't your nature to give up. Your character is to fight. As you once wrote, strife is your meat and drink; you've got to fight.' And again it went for me, and said: 'Tomorrow morning get out of this bed. No matter what you feel like, get out of this bed. You needn't put your clothes on, just put a dressing gown on, and DO something. Start checking what you have written. Get onto the tape.' [I always start my books on tape.]

And I said, 'But I'm too ill to get up.'

And the voice said, 'We know how ill you are, but you tell Tom of your decision.'

And I said, 'I haven't made a decision.'

'But you have...'

And this went on for about an hour.

The next morning I told Tom exactly what had happened. I told him the exact words because it was still so fresh, and Tom said, 'Yes, that's right, you know, this is what you should do.'

I could hardly stand on my feet but I got up and stayed up for half a day. And when I got back into bed, as always with my tape recorder beside me, I mumbled into it, 'Sarah, I'm not sure where I was in this story, but start a new chapter.' [It had been three months since I had written a word of it.] And then, 'I know what has to happen. Start a new chapter...' And from there, it went on...

This morning I don't feel any joy but I have an idea for a story which is the next best thing.

Lord, beckon me to joy:
My mind is weary
My body sick;
Who can I employ
To ease my spirit
And lift my heart
And give me strength
To combat this strife
And the energy
To work at life?
Lord, beckon me to joy.
I have no hobbies:
No more do I knit,
Play the piano or paint;
My mind abhors the needle,
My fingers irritate the keys,
I see no colours, no trees.
Then what do I do
With my days?
I write,
And part of the night.
O Lord, beckon me to joy.

EPILOGUE

The author describes her novels as 'readable social history interwoven into the lives of people', but that disguises her art. It is precisely how history is woven into the lives of people that sets apart talented writers in the genre from the rest of the field. Many historical novels are full of history and empty of character; some others are peopled by characters who would be more at home in the twentieth century

Catherine does not write historical plots to order; thank goodness, she would not know how to. Her talent is as creator, as life-giver to real characters who are made to exist in our imagination. Her readers know what it is to be ensnared by a master storyteller, to be led breathless from one scene to the next. But she achieves this through the most complete presentation of character: we believe in her people and can imagine what they would feel in any situation. As the *New York Times Book Review* recently said about *The Black Velvet Gown*, 'Mrs Cookson treats her characters and their problems as Thomas Hardy or Elizabeth Cleghorn Gaskell would – that is, omnisciently.' Their stories cannot help but unfold.

Whence do her people come? Today, in the fine and tasteful surroundings of this millionairess's Langley home it is hauntingly possible to catch a glimpse of the little girl from Leam Lane, held hostage in a 'fortress of pain wherein she was a child'. She stands centre stage in the kitchen of the house in William Black Street, listening, absorbing and – incredibly, aged seven – feeling responsible for the lives and relationships of a granda, a grandma, an uncle called Jack, and a mother we now know as our Kate.

'Everything that happened in that kitchen,' she says, 'everything I thought, everything that I have written since seems to have been bred in that kitchen.'

The South Tyneside Council plays host to thousands who come, even from America, to the environment that engendered her people: to see the plaques at William Black Street, St Peter & Paul's, the Workhouse (now the General Hospital), Rory's boatyard or Westoe Village where he first called on Charlotte Kean with her father's slum rents, or Shields Market that once witnessed Mrs McGrath's vicious assault on Tilly Trotter's infant son, or Jarrow, where Bede's ancient church contains a table made by the hunger marchers of the '30s, and which is redolent today with memories of Palmer's great shipyard and the long, remarkable life of Katie Mulholland. And now in South Shields' Ocean Road Museum, that kitchen itself: 'the hub, the heart of the matter, the axis about which revolved the lives of my people, be they what they may...'

Significantly, *My Land of the North* provides in the passages from her writings a map of the author no less than that of the area and its people, but only the full scope of her novels can illustrate the complexities of the woman. The part of her character most commonly to the fore in Katie Mulholland and Tilly Trotter has largely been subsumed, though two other characters are still embattled within her: Mary Ann, the 'holy innocent', and Miss Brigmore, embodiment of high moral principles (though happily flawed). In the continuing battle Mary Ann as the little liar still maintains the upper hand, just as she did when Catherine was a child. 'It was me granda who first told me I was a writer. He didn't actually say I was a writer, not in so many words... I can see myself running up the backyard and into the kitchen and going straight for him where he sat in his chair, crying, "Granda! you know that little man you tell me about, the one that sits on the wall in Ireland no bigger than your hand, you know him? With the green jacket and the red trousers and the buckle on his shoes, and the high hat and a shillelagh as big as himself, you remember, Granda?"

"Aye, what about him?"

"Well, I've seen him, Granda."

"Ya have?"

"Aye, Granda. He was round the top corner."

"He was, was he? And I suppose he spoke to you?"

"Aye, Granda, he did."

"And what did he say?"

"Well, he said, 'Hello Katie.'"

"He said, 'Hello Katie,' did he? And what did you say?"

"...I said, 'Hello Mister, me granda knows you.'"

He wiped his tash with his hand while raising his white eyebrows, then he said: "You know what you are, Katie McMullen, don't ya? You're a stinking liar. But go on, go on, don't stop, for begod! it will get you some place... Either into clink or into the money!'"

The philosopher, the moralist, the teacher loom large, but the natural storyteller is still in the lead.

Catherine's belief that she inherited from her father genes which somehow set her apart from the hopelessness around her not only fostered the strength to work hard but also, in rare moments of freedom, to strive to be better herself. Her father 'provided the norm at which I aimed. Without that side of me,' she believes, 'I may not have become a writer.' This selective self-image 'pushed and pulled' her out of the early environment of poverty and stigma, and she left the North East. It is impossible to read of Sarah's impoverished family in *The Blind Miller* 'wallowing and choking in a sea of mud like that which filled the timber yard at Jarrow Slake', and not wonder what it took Catherine to perform her own rescue from the mire.

In Hastings the angst that her 'escape' produced possibly hastened the breakdown that lasted ten years. Whether it was this, the unremitting work, the trauma of the loss of her children in childbirth, the inner turbulence aggravated by her growing disaffection with Catholicism, or a combination of all that lay at its root, it was neither the Church nor even Lord Chesterfield who drew her slowly up from the hell into which she had fallen, but Tom Cookson.

With Tom's help she began to accept her roots and 'throw off the pseudo-lady'. What emerged was a true novelist of the spirit, yet far from the Romantic tradition. In *The Mallen Litter* Catherine writes: 'Neither the events of the world nor the struggles of the working class towards emancipation touched Brook House and its inmates during these years. Mrs Dan Benshaw occupied herself mostly with reading the works of the Bronte sisters, never Dickens or Mrs Gaskell.' It is nigh on certain that Catherine and Barbara Bensham would not have seen eye to eye had they met, and who knows perhaps they did!

The saying that you cannot tell a book by its cover has never been more literally true than in her case. There is nothing sentimental about her writing; Catherine is unrelenting in the strong images she employs to cast her spell. They are born of her formative years and her struggle to realise herself. No one who has read even one of her books (and there are few who can have stopped at one) can visit Tyneside without hearing the sounds of the steelworks, the hubbub of the now silent docks, or the voices of her characters as they once passed through the halls of her imagination and now live on in ours.

As the traveller crosses the Tyne between Gateshead and Newcastle, nature and the works of man combine to excite our wonderment and awe. This is the gateway, you feel, to the capital of another kingdom, but it is also the focal point of Catherine Cookson's country: the Tyne is its binding factor, the reason for prosperity in its heyday and now imbued with the moods and tempers cast upon it by Catherine's tales, tales which ring true for readers from all over the world. Catherine's insight into the lives of ordinary

As the traveller crosses the Tyne between Gateshead and Newcastle, nature and the works of man combine to excite our wonderment and awe. This is the gateway, you feel, to the capital of another kingdom, but it is also the focal point of Catherine Cookson's country: the Tyne is its binding factor,

people is so exceptional that she is translated into seventeen different languages and read in all English-speaking countries, but as she says, 'Human nature is much the same the world over.'

The integrity of her spirit, now assured by the reunion with the environment that inspired it, is today enhanced by her determination to give spiritually, emotionally and financially to those in need. Her warmth and generosity permeate her books and are very probably another factor in their extraordinary popularity. On her eightieth birthday, the date on which this book was first published, she showed herself as indefatigable as ever. In hospital one day for a distressing operation, she would be back in her beautiful home the next, propped up in bed by pillows, not languishing but embarked upon yet another novel, destined like all the others to become a bestseller.

INDEX

ACKNOWLEDGEMENTS

The author would like to thank all the picture sources. The colour maps are by ML Design, the black and white photographs by kind permission of Hulton Getty Picture Library, the Beamish North of England Open Air Museum, the Bede Gallery, the Borough of South Tyneside, Brian Duff, Gateshead Libraries & Arts Dept, the Gibson Collection, *The Newcastle Journal*, the Newcastle University Library, North Tyneside Libraries & Arts Dept, the Northumberland Record Office, Paul Perry, Vince Rea, Fred Mudditt, Edward Cowen, and the *South Shields Gazette*.
Colour stills from the films of *Tilly Trotter* and *Colour Blind*, *The Dwelling Place*, *The Girl*, *The Glass Virgin* and *The Gambling Man*, all photographed by Moira Conway, are reproduced by kind permission of Festival Film & TV Ltd. The still from *The Fifteen Streets* is reproduced by kind permission of Tyne Tees Television.
All other colour photography is by Piers Dudgeon, with thanks to Cedric Bilverston of the North East Boating Federation and Brian Thompson, who, respectively, supplied and piloted the boat. While every effort has been made to trace copyright sources, the publishers would be grateful to hear from any unacknowledged copyright holders.